SIR EDWYN HOSKYNS
AS A BIBLICAL THEOLOGIAN

Following the publication of *Lux Mundi* in 1889, Anglican biblical scholars, mainly from the Catholic tradition, were in the forefront of critical studies. Sir Edwyn Clement Hoskyns was one such scholar. This book sets out to place Hoskyns against the background of his own time, both in Cambridge, where he spent most of his working life, and the various movements in theology such as Liberal Protestantism and Catholic Modernism.

Naturally biblical study has developed since Hoskyns' time, but this book argues that many of the issues which he raised still have importance, such as the continuity between Jesus and the Church, and Jesus at the centre of the Christian tradition. Hoskyns' commentary on the Fourth Gospel remains classic, and today scholars and preachers alike are returning to the stands he took.

Richard E. Parsons, born in 1946, is a priest of the Church of England. He was successively a tutor at the Church Army Training College and a Selection Secretary with the Advisory Council for the Church's Ministry (ACCM) before becoming Vicar of the large London parish of Hendon in 1984.

Sir Edwyn Hoskyns

Richard E. Parsons

Sir Edwyn Hoskyns
as a Biblical Theologian

C. HURST & COMPANY, LONDON
ST. MARTIN'S PRESS, NEW YORK

First published in the United Kingdom by
C. Hurst & Co. (Publishers) Ltd.,
38 King Street, London WC2E 8JT,
and in the United States of America by
St. Martin's Press, Inc.,
175 Fifth Avenue, New York, NY 10010.
Printed in England

ISBNs

Hurst: 1–85065–017–9
St. Martin's: 0–312–72647–3

Library of Congress Cataloging-in-Publication Data

Parsons, Richard E.
    Sir Edwyn Hoskyns as a biblical theologian.

    "The published works of Sir Edwyn Hoskins": p.
    Bibliography: p.
    Includes index.
    1. Hoskyns, Edwyn Clement, Sir, 1884–1937.
2. Bible. N.T.--Criticism, interpretation, etc.--History
--20th century. I. Title.
BS2351.H67P37 1985   220'.092'4   85–25038
ISBN 0–312–72647–3

In memory of
Stanley John Ashby
1920–1981

FOREWORD

The fact that the centenary of the birth of Sir Edwyn Hoskyns in 1884 has recently passed is not of itself sufficient justification for a study of his thought. Yet with the enormous interest now generated for the period between the two world wars it seems pertinent to record the contribution of one scholar to biblical study during that period. This provided a background against which subsequent scholarship came to develop — and to which it ought on occasions to return. Therefore it is indeed a hasty judgement to dismiss Hoskyns' contribution automatically as 'dated'.

This study was written during the time that I was a Lecturer at the Church Army Training College, a Selection Secretary with the Advisory Council for the Church's Ministry and an honorary assistant curate at All Saints' Blackheath in the Diocese of Southwark. I am grateful to all the audiences who patiently listened to my views on Hoskyns, sometimes daily. The Vicar of All Saints' Blackheath, Canon Stanley John Ashby, sadly died when this essay was about to be completed. I am grateful to him for enormous help and encouragement over this work and much else, and for that reason I dedicate it to his memory.

Professor Christopher Evans was a marvellous supervisor and I thank the University of London for the award of the degree of Master of Philosophy as a result of it. I am indebted to the Revd Gordon Wakefield, the Revd Richard Gutteridge and in particular to Mary, Lady Hoskyns for so generously discussing the subject with me on many occasions. My wife Elaine was wonderfully supportive throughout the project and without her love and patience this study could never have seen the light of day. My friend the Revd Christopher Bedford also gave enthusiastic support, and some of the final revision was done at his Rectory in Bethnal Green. My thanks go, finally, to the Revd Grant Holmes for reading the proofs and helping in the preparation of the index.

September 1985   R.E.P.

CONTENTS

ABBREVIATIONS

B.J.R.L.	*Bulletin of the John Rylands Library*
C.Q.R.	*Church Quarterly Review*
D.N.B.	*Dictionary of National Biography*
Exp. T.	*Expository Times*
H.T.R.	*Harvard Theological Review*
J.C.H.	*Journal of Contemporary History*
J.E.H.	*Journal of Ecclesiastical History*
J.T.S.	*Journal of Theological Studies*
Nov. T.	*Novum Testamentum*
N.T.S.	*New Testament Studies*
S.B.T.	Studies in Biblical Theology
S.E.	*Studia Evangelica*
S.J.T.	*Scottish Journal of Theology*
S.P.C.K.	Society for Promoting Christian Knowledge

Use is made of the following abbreviated titles of books referred to frequently in the notes:

Cambridge Sermons	Hoskyns, E.C., *Cambridge Sermons* (1938).
The Fourth Gospel	Hoskyns, E.C. (F.N. Davey, ed.), *The Fourth Gospel*, 1 vol., 2nd edn (1947).
Gore to Temple	Ramsey, A.M., *From Gore to Temple* (1961).
Modernist Movement	Vidler, A.R., *The Modernist Movement in the Roman Church: Its Origins and Outcome* (1934).
The Riddle of the New Testament	Hoskyns, E.C., and F.N. Davey, *The Riddle of the New Testament* (1931).
20th Century Defenders	Vidler, A.R., *20th Century Defenders of the Faith* (1965).
Wörterbuch	Kittel, G. (ed.), *Theologisches Wörterbuch zum Neuen Testament* (1932) — subsequently edited by G. Friedrich. Also commonly designated as *T.W.N.T.* Eng. transl. *Theological Dictionary of the New Testament*.

INTRODUCTION

Sir Edwyn Clement Hoskyns, eleventh baronet, acted as Dean of Corpus Christi College, Cambridge, from 1919 until his untimely death in June 1937. Originally appointed in 1916, he went off to serve as an Army chaplain and was awarded the Military Cross (the commanding officer of his battalion, the 7th Manchesters, referred to him in a book of memoirs published many years later as 'an exemplary padre'). During his time as Dean he established for himself a considerable reputation as a biblical scholar, teacher, preacher and priest.[1] This essay is concerned with his contribution to biblical studies and with some of the questions raised by him especially in relation to the New Testament.

Hoskyns managed to combine many cross-currents in his theology. When a student, he had listened to Adolf Harnack's lectures in Berlin and as a result favoured the alternative position of Catholic Modernism, especially as represented by its principal biblical scholar, Alfred Loisy. He became a friend of Albert Schweitzer and understood him well.[2] He was deeply interested in German scholarship, attending three conferences of Anglo-German theologians in Canterbury, Wartburg and Chichester respectively and contributing an essay 'Jesus the Messiah' in the volume *Mysterium Christi* published after the Wartburg conference. He became interested also in the developing movement in theology to discuss the major biblical works, and introduced into England[3] the influential multi-volume *Theologisches Wörterbuch zum Neuen Testament*, edited by his friend Gerhard Kittel.

In religion Hoskyns was always an Anglican Catholic, following in the particular tradition of John Keble. He spoke on three occasions[4] to Anglo-Catholic congresses, giving addresses on 'Christ and Catholicism', 'The Eucharist in the New Testament' and 'The Apostolicity of the Church'. He contributed an essay, 'The Christ of the Synoptic Gospels', in the volume *Essays Catholic and Critical*, edited by E.G. Selwyn.

Perhaps, after all, Hoskyns will be remembered for his interest in Karl Barth's theology; his translation of Barth's commentary on the Epistle to the Romans was published in 1933. This interest in Barth will have to be carefully analysed as it is often more subtle than is frequently supposed. In 1936 Hoskyns wrote an open letter to Barth[5] and the significance of this letter is probably in what it does not say rather than in its contents, thus giving us little clue as to what Hoskyns thought about Barth's later work.

1

The crown of Hoskyns' writings was his commentary on the Fourth Gospel. His writing of this was interrupted by his translation of Barth's commentary and, as a result, the final form of the commentary was not as he would have wished it to be at the time of his death.[6] It was edited by one of his pupils, Francis Noel Davey. Hoskyns and Davey had already collaborated in the writing of Hoskyns' first book *The Riddle of the New Testament*, published in 1931, and its sequel *Crucifixion-Resurrection*, finally published fifty years later.

The concern of this essay is not with Hoskyns' life — already admirably covered by Gordon Wakefield in his editorial introduction to *Crucifixion-Resurrection* — but rather with the way in which he monitored various movements in biblical interpretation.

English theology has gained the reputation of being insular, and English students of being mere babes in 'critical' studies. Hoskyns' influence told against this, especially in relation to Germany. He introduced into England the works of German scholars, reviewed German books, translated German theological writings, spoke constantly to Cambridge students about German scholars many of whom he knew personally, participated in international conferences, and encouraged his students to spend time in German universities. Thus it will be necessary to assess the influence of German theology upon English scholarship and to discuss the measure and nature of that influence. Hoskyns remained, as did others, an Anglican Catholic biblical scholar at a time when Roman Catholic biblical scholarship had been limited by papal intervention.[7] Thus it was in Anglican circles that the bible was interpreted 'critically' but within a Catholic framework.

In the opening chapter we shall discuss this ecclesiastical background against which he was working. In the chapter which follows, an analysis of the twin influences of 'Liberal Catholicism' and continental, especially German, theology upon Hoskyns' own theological development will be attempted. In the remaining chapters his theological work up to 1931, *The Riddle of the New Testament*, and his commentary on the Fourth Gospel, interrupted by his translation of Barth's *Romans*, will be considered in turn. In the concluding chapter we shall attempt to explore further the character and validity of Hoskyns' work on the Fourth Gospel by considering it in relation to the work of subsequent writers on that Gospel and their attitude to and use of his commentary.

Hoskyns wrote just before the high-water mark of the so-called biblical theology epoch,[8] but it is doubtful if he would have accepted the 'system' which this approach later developed and which may explain why it became increasingly unfashionable. Hoskyns, however, by his writing and teaching, has raised questions which students of the New Testament ought not to ignore. It is interesting that he has been recently linked to the growing concern among some New Testament scholars today that the New Testament writings need to be studied from both the theological and the historical points of view.[9]

NOTES

1. Sir Gerald Hurst, *Closed Chapters*, Manchester, 1942, p. 82; F.L. Cross and E. Livingstone (ed.), *The Oxford Dictionary of the Christian Church*, 2nd edn, Oxford, 1974, p. 669; *D.N.B. 1931–1940*, Oxford, 1949, pp. 448f.; *Cambridge Sermons*, pp. vii–xxviii; C.H. Smyth, 'In Memoriam: Canon Sir Edwyn Hoskyns, 1884–1937', *Theology*, XXXV, 1937, pp. 135–41; *The Times*, 30 June 1937, obituary notice; J.O. Cobham, 'E.C. Hoskyns: The Sunderland Curate', *C.Q.R.*, CLVIII, 1957, pp. 280–95.
2. C.K. Barrett, 'Albert Schweitzer and the New Testament', *Exp. T.*, LXXXVII, 1975, p. 4.
3. 'A Theological Lexicon to the New Testament', *Theology*, XXVI, 1933, pp. 82–7.
4. *Christ and Catholicism*, Anglo-Catholic Congress Books, 12, 1923; 'The Eucharist and the New Testament', Anglo-Catholic Congress Report, 1927, pp. 51–6; 'The Apostolicity of the Church', Anglo-Catholic Congress Report, 1930, pp. 85–90.
5. *Cambridge Sermons*, pp. 217–21.
6. *The Fourth Gospel*, pp. 5–11.
7. B.M.G. Reardon, *Roman Catholic Modernism*, London, 1970, pp. 237–48.
8. *20th Century Defenders*, pp. 88–100; *Gore to Temple*, pp. 129–45.
9. Note R.H. Fuller's Presidential Address 'Sir Edwyn Hoskyns and the Contemporary Relevance of "Biblical Theology"', delivered to Studiorum Novi Testamenti Societas, *N.T.S.*, 30, July 1984; also G.N. Stanton's editorial 'The Passing of an Era?', *N.T.S.*, 30, 1984, p. 2.

1

BACKGROUND DEVELOPMENTS

The contribution of Sir Edwyn Hoskyns to biblical studies in the 1920s and 1930s must be set against the background of the theological thought of his time with special reference to the University of Cambridge where he worked. To a greater extent than before or since, theological thought in the Church of England, and to some extent in Britain outside the Church of England, was governed in the first three decades of the twentieth century by movements associated with parties. Each of these parties had a wide spectrum and, as is generally the case, some of their members were only loosely attached to them, while there were many who refused allegiance to any party. Nevertheless, a good deal of theological work was done under the aegis of party affiliations, and for this reason was often accompanied by acute controversy. The parties may be designated Liberal Catholic, Liberal Protestant and Modernist.

The Liberal Catholics were heirs of the Catholic revival in the Church of England stemming from the Oxford Movement and its protagonists, the Tractarians. The term 'Liberal Catholic', however, indicated that a change and development had taken place. Theologically Tractarians had been traditionalist and conservative in relation both to doctrine and the Bible, none more so than their chief biblical scholar, E.B. Pusey, Regius Professor of Hebrew at Oxford from 1828 till his death in 1882. Two visits to Germany in his youth had given him a deeper knowledge of and, for the time being, some sympathy with what was then being talked about as 'the scientific spirit' and 'a new era in theology'.[1] But later he turned his back on this, as can be seen in one of his best known works in biblical scholarship, a course of lectures on the Book of Daniel. Here he amassed the arguments for the traditional date and authorship of the book, in opposition to the ascription of it to an unknown author in the age of the Maccabees. His scholarship and exegesis had a massive quality informed by his knowledge of the Fathers,[2] but he remained to the end of his life deeply conservative, and under his leadership the Tractarian party was as resolutely opposed as were the Evangelicals to the first appearances of what came to be known as 'Higher Criticism'. This attitude of mind was confirmed by H.P. Liddon, from 1870 Dean Ireland Professor at Oxford. In his Bampton lectures, published in 1867, entitled *The*

Divinity of our Lord, he sought to maintain the strictest standards of orthodoxy without the slightest concession to the difficulties then being raised by biblical criticism.

It was, however, from a Tractarian stable that an attempt was made to unite Catholicism with the development of scientific thought and biblical criticism and to show that they were not necessarily incompatible. This was made in the collection of essays by a number of Oxford scholars entitled *Lux Mundi*, published in 1889. The editor, also the author of the most important and controversial essay 'The Holy Spirit and Inspiration', was Charles Gore, and an indication of the break which this book made is the fact that after its publication Liddon did not speak to his friend Gore again. But what Liddon regarded as a betrayal of the orthodox faith many in the Catholic tradition of the Church of England were to regard as a positive step forward and a great liberation, and it was later to be seen as a landmark in the history of theological thought[3] and 'a new era in Anglican thought'.[4] Thus '*Lux Mundi* marks a turning point in the theology of the Catholic revival';[5] it also 'marked a great step forward in so far as it delivered Christians from the desperate duty of ignoring the scientific teaching of the modern world'.[6] Further, one of its lasting effects was 'the inauguration of a series of commentaries on the books of the Bible, which aims at combining a hearty acceptance of critical principles with loyalty to the Catholic Faith (the 'Westminster Commentaries'), W. Lock being its first editor.'[7]

Gore's aim, which may already have been conceived when he was teaching the Bible to ordinands at Cuddesdon,[8] was to confront the reader with the implications of biblical criticism for the historic faith. The theme of the Holy Spirit and Inspiration is set within the context of historical theology, the essay being full of patristic references. The life-giving work of the Holy Spirit is said to be ever active in the human race. Man is a social being who cannot realise himself in isolation, and yet all the while the Spirit nourishes individuality. The Spirit works gradually, moulding sinful human nature to the divine will, and within the Church man is helped to grow in patience. From a description of the work of the Spirit within the Church, Gore leads on to a discussion of the Holy Spirit and the Bible. To believe in the inspiration of Scripture is to put oneself to school with every part of the Old Testament as of the New. It is the record of the Spirit at work in the unique redemptive process in Israel.

If this is the case, how is it possible for criticism to suggest that the story of Jonah is mere parable in the face of our Lord's citation of it as history or to query the Davidic authorship of Psalm 110 in the face of our Lord's citation of it as Davidic? Gore argued that the conclusions of biblical scholarship must stand; Christ was infallible in what he deliberately revealed concerning God and man, but his revelation was given through human nature, and so Christ participated in the state of knowledge of his time. Christ did not anticipate the findings of science or criticism; his knowledge as man was limited. In Gore's own words: 'He willed so to restrain the beams of His Deity as to observe the limits of the science of His age, and He put Himself in the same relationship to its historical knowledge.'[9] Gore's general conclusions at this point are that it is impossible to maintain the historicity of the Old Testament at all points, that Jesus himself spoke as a Jew of his century, that the New Testament may contain errors of detail; but that the historical framework of the Bible is nevertheless entirely trustworthy and of the Holy Spirit. Gore then, through his *Lux Mundi* essay, 'delivered many in one section of the Church of England, and possibly others also, from the alternatives of obscurantism or unbelief: and it was part of the strength of that essay that he refused to treat the question of inspiration until he had first written at length about the Holy Spirit.'[10]

Gore also established himself as a leader in biblical criticism, but he did not continue to be so later. The reasons for this are well expressed in a letter written by Hoskyns: 'Gore was one of the pioneers in accepting the critical approach to the study of the Bible. Later on he seemed to have allowed the right of the critic up to a certain point after which Gore became rigid, and was apt to be harsh. Personally, I think this was not because he really refused to see what his own critical principles involved but because he genuinely thought certain results were sound, and others cranky and critically doubtful. But whatever the cause, at the end Gore did draw a line through the critical movement which meant that he ceased to be a leader in Biblical exegesis.'[11]

This judgement marks a further development in Liberal Catholicism[12] in which the approach to biblical studies became more radical, and, following the spirit of Catholic Modernism,[13] more consideration was given to the place of experience in theology. Gore would not have wholly approved of this development.

The changes noted appear in a comparison between *Lux Mundi* and the later volume of essays entitled *Essays Catholic and Critical*, published in 1926 under the editorship of E.G. Selwyn. In the preface Selwyn acknowledged his debt to the authors of *Lux Mundi*, and in many ways the aims of the two volumes were similar, namely to bring the Catholic and critical movements into a synthesis and to attempt a fresh exposition and defence of the Catholic faith. But in other ways the situation had changed. There was now a far greater use of biblical criticism and less reliance on an exclusively historical method, but *Essays Catholic and Critical* lacked 'the grasp of dogmatic wholeness and the depth of moral intensity'[14] found in the earlier volume. Certainly *Essays Catholic and Critical* was to be a most important volume for the advancement of Liberal Catholicism, as H.L. Stewart noted: 'In *Essays Catholic and Critical* we have before uᶜ at its best what the Anglo-Catholic Movement means today.'[15] But the book is now less well known because the days of Liberal Catholicism are past,[16] and partly because its style was so unattractive.

The scope of the book was wide, including both biblical and systematic theology. The contributors, though not a homogeneous group, were for the most part to become, if they had not already become, influential theologians in their own fields. The contributors, therefore, fall roughly into two groups: those who were already well-known theological writers and those younger scholars who were embarking on major theological writing for the first time. The editor E.G. Selwyn, also the author of the article on 'The Resurrection', had been editor since 1920 of *Theology*, which had become something of a platform for biblical Catholicism, and was eventually to produce a massive commentary on 1 Peter (1946). A.E.J. Rawlinson, who wrote on 'Authority as a Ground of Belief', had already made his mark with his outstanding commentary on Mark in the 'Westminster Commentaries' (1925) and his Bampton Lectures (1926) on *The New Testament Doctrine of Christ*. He was to continue to write on biblical and later ecumenical subjects. A.E. Taylor, writing on 'The Vindication of Religion', had already gained a considerable reputation as a philosopher of religion. W.L. Knox, probably the most learned of them all, had already produced *St Paul and the Church of Jerusalem* (1925) and was to continue his thorough and outstanding scholarship with *St Paul and the Church of the Gentiles* (1939), *Some Hellenistic Elements in Primitive Christianity*, the Schweich Lectures on Biblical Archaeology in 1942 (1944), lectures on the Acts of the Apostles (1948), and later *The Sources of the Synoptic Gospels* (published posthumously; vol. I 1953 and vol. II 1957). For some, as for Hoskyns himself, this was their first important piece of theological writing and was followed by major works of scholarship.

N.P. Williams, writing on 'The Origins of the Sacraments', was later to produce a major work, *The Ideas of the Fall and of Original Sin* (1927). K.E. Kirk, writing on 'The Atonement', was later to write on Christian Ethics, especially *The Vision of God* (1931), and on the Epistle to the Romans (1937). Here and there in the volume, and notably in W. Spens' contribution on the Eucharist, as previously in his full-scale work *Belief and Practice* (1915), there can be observed influences from the Catholic Modernist movement, stressing particularly at this point Christian experience as evidence for the construction of doctrine. W.R. Matthews expressed this as follows: 'Anglo-Catholic theologians have been and are among the most distinguished and sometimes the most drastic of Biblical critics; and the Modernism of Loisy and Tyrrell, driven underground in the Roman Church, has found a congenial home in Anglo-Catholic theology.'[17]

Two years after the appearance of *Essays Catholic and Critical*, the biblical critical side of Liberal Catholicism, and hence the strength of the movement at the time, was to be seen in the appearance of a one-volume commentary on the whole Bible, entitled *A New Commentary on Holy Scripture including the Apocrypha* (1928). It was edited by C. Gore, H.L. Goudge and A. Guillaume, and among its contributors were many who had contributed to *Essays Catholic and Critical* — Hoskyns on the Johannine Epistles, Knox on Galatians, N.P. Williams on Romans, J.K. Mozley on 1 and 2 Corinthians, Selwyn on the evidence of the Resurrection, E.G. Bicknell on the functions of literary and historical criticism, and with an introduction to the Wisdom Literature and the Acts of the Apostles, while E.O. James wrote an essay on a Comparative Study of the Old Testament. The approach was outlined in the preface: 'This commentary is written by Anglican scholars who, while holding their faith, are determined in approaching the books to give their critical faculty, instructed by all the means within their power, its full and rightful freedom. It is hardly necessary to say that they have not found the results of legitimate criticism to conflict with the Catholic faith . . . their conclusions do very often differ widely from those which have been traditional.' However, the *New Commentary* was certainly conservative by modern standards, and editorial notes were added at intervals to correct what the Editors regarded as an unduly critical point of view. Knox and Vidler, summing up the approach of the commentary, noted that it 'marks a half-way house between history as evidence for the truth of Christianity and the view that the Catholic religion is a fact which is evidence for the truth of the narratives which describe its origin.'[18]

Ramsey saw it as 'a final monument of the conservatively critical scholarship of which *Lux Mundi* had been the harbinger some forty years before'.[19]

The Liberal Protestants[20] also formed a strong party within the Church of England, but they were not as important or influential in the field of biblical studies as the Liberal Catholics. The Liberal Protestants were historically descended from the Evangelical party, who had been prominent in the Victorian church. Generally the Evangelicals were as opposed as the traditional Catholics to biblical criticism; in 1901, for example, at a meeting of the National Council of Evangelical Free Churches at Cardiff, Professor Rendel Harris was shouted off the platform having referred mildly to the origins of the book of Genesis. The next year, there appeared a book by Sir Robert Anderson entitled *The Bible and Modern Criticism*; with a preface by Bishop Handley Moule of Durham, it was little more than a sweeping denunciation of the biblical critics. A volume of essays was produced by Liberal Evangelicals (edited by J.R. Houden), but this was not well known. Some concessions were made to biblical criticism as seen from a remark by G.T. Manley in his essay 'The Inspiration and Authority of the Bible': 'The evidence adduced by science, by archaeology, and by literary criticism goes to strengthen rather than to weaken our faith in the Bible' (p. 153). This would give weight to a comment of L.E. Elliott-Binns that 'the Evangelicals, though many would have been loath to admit it, were much more Liberal and were moving steadily in that direction,'[21] and as a result much of the power of Liberal Protestantism was to be found in the English Modernist movement.

The English Modernists formed a distinguishable and a distinguished group within the Church of England. They formed the Churchmen's Union in 1898 (later to be called the Modern Churchmen's Union), and Hastings Rashdall became its first President. Some of the most formidable of English theologians belonged to it: for example R.H. Charles, J.M. Creed, W. Sanday, F. Jackson, K. Lake, P. Gardner, W.R. Inge, H.J.A. Major, H. Rashdall, C.E. Raven, B.H. Streeter and J.F. Bethune-Baker. Among these were expert biblical scholars, yet although they were called Modernists it is likely that it was Liberal Protestant assumptions which influenced many of the English Modern Churchmen.[22] Vidler characterises them as 'a group of highly gifted individuals without a positive common mind or any such popular following as to constitute a fashion'.[23] They were against theological obscurantism, and most of them disliked Anglo-Catholicism. Although they shared many of the assumptions of Liberal Protestantism, and indeed W.R. Inge severely criticised Catholic Modernism,[24] they were never so theologically radical as the pure Liberal Protestants, perhaps because they were attached to the *Book of Common Prayer* and to the establishment of the Church of England. Percy Gardner sums up their general outlook: 'Before a great constructive period in the history of thought there is always an invading wave of scepticism, which is in the minds of the great thinkers of the time, clears away much of the traditional beliefs, and leaves a platform for the erection of a new fabric of faith.'[25]

What was this new fabric of faith and what did the English Modernists wish to retain as the essence of Christian theology? Here again it should be noted that they had no overall distinctive theology but were a group committed to reform. Individual Modernists were, however, to make great contributions to biblical scholarship. The oldest was William Sanday of Oxford[26] whose position, advanced at some points and conservative at others, was not reached until 1912, from which date until his death he was involved in controversy, especially with Charles Gore.[27] Sanday held a unique position among English theologians of the time as an interpreter of foreign New Testament scholarship. His *Life of Christ in Recent Research* sketched the rise of the eschatological school of interpretation of the Gospels, and with Professor F.C. Burkitt of Cambridge he welcomed the work of Albert Schweitzer, saying of his work that he 'keeps much closer to the texts than most critics do. . . . He does not, like so many critics, seek to reduce the person of Christ to the common measure of humanity, but leaves it at the transcendental heights. . . .'[28] Encouraged then by Burkitt and Sanday, many English scholars read Schweitzer and were led to a conviction that the mysterious and catastrophic elements cannot be eliminated from the record of Jesus, and that for all their difficulty they provide a bridge between him and apostolic Christianity.[29]

Sanday also organised a seminar which met fortnightly during term. Some of the volumes of the *International Critical Commentary* may have arisen from this seminar, especially Sanday's own commentary on Romans written in collaboration with A.C. Headlam, and that on Matthew by W.C. Allen. In 1911 the group published a volume of essays entitled *Oxford Studies in the Synoptic Problem*, which dealt with various aspects of the Synoptic Problem in great detail. It was Sanday's hope to write a *magnum opus* on the life of Christ, but this was never fulfilled.

A prominent member of Sanday's seminar was B.H. Streeter

(1874–1937). For Streeter religious faith was always a quest, and since his contribution to the volume *Foundations* in 1912 he had frequently been attacked as a Modernist.[30] He was to make a notable contribution to technical biblical scholarship in his Bampton Lectures *The Four Gospels: A Study of Origins* (1924). In his contribution to *Oxford Studies in the Synoptic Problem*, Streeter had argued for the priority of Mark and for the existence of 'Q'. In his later volume he expounded a number of new ideas, notably in the first section relating to textual criticism and the Caesarean text, and especially later on the composition of Luke's Gospel. He argued that this Gospel had appeared, or had been prepared, in two different stages: first by the combination of the material of 'Q' with material which is peculiar to Luke in one single document, which Streeter called Proto-Luke;[31] and later by the combination, by the same writer or another, of this already existing Gospel with certain selections from Mark.[32] This work, detailed and persuasively argued, became a standard textbook for New Testament students, and many of the conclusions came to be widely accepted. It represented 'a comprehensive gathering together of the results of the scientific study of the Gospels up till that time'.[33] The book, however, had its weaknesses. It attempted to cover too much ground: the problems of New Testament manuscript tradition, the Synoptic relationships and the Fourth Gospel (this section was much weaker than the others) are pressed together into one volume. It was primarily a masterly summary of the previous fifty or so years of New Testament research, and it neither broke much new ground nor raised any strictly theological questions; indeed, many were surprised that Streeter's conclusions were so 'conservative', the Gospels being accepted as reliable historical documents and, in some cases, given early dates of composition.

Modernist biblical scholarship of a different kind was the contribution to *Cambridge Biblical Essays* (ed. H.B. Swete, 1909) by W.R. Inge[34] on the theology of the Fourth Gospel. Inge was sympathetic to platonic spirituality, and this had found expression in his Bampton Lectures of 1899, entitled *Christian Mysticism*. His account of the theology of the Fourth Gospel is linked with this interest in philosophical mysticism. 'The Fourth Gospel is not a philosophical treatise,' he wrote, 'but it rests on a philosophy of life, which we must understand if we wish to understand the book. Its chief characteristics are Idealism, Mysticism, and Symbolism.'[35] The mystical element in religion was for him primary, and he believed that the essence of the Christian religion was separate from the traditional scheme of dogma and institution.

The detailed critical work of Kirsopp Lake[36] and F.J. Foakes-Jackson[37] may also be placed within the English Modernist school, though it was later to become an embarrassment to the Modernists.[38] In his early years Lake had written two provocative New Testament books: *Historical Evidence for the Resurrection of Jesus Christ* (1907), which challenged the sufficiency of the evidence of the empty tomb, and *Earlier Epistles of St Paul* (1911), which maintained that the course of primitive Christianity was profoundly affected by the influence of the mystery religions. Foakes-Jackson had been for the greater part of his career a Fellow of Jesus College, Cambridge, but in 1916 had moved to the United States where he combined with Lake to edit the first three volumes of *The Beginnings of Christianity* (1920–33), Lake editing the last two volumes alone. The first volume, produced with the collaboration of a considerable team of English and American scholars, was intended to initiate a critical and historical examination of Christian origins, and it included an investigation of the historical traditions concerning Jesus. The general conclusion was that the religion of the apostolic age was a sacramental Catholicism, but when the accretions made by the early Church were pruned away, Jesus emerged with a prophetic and ethical message. Foakes-Jackson's paper, given at the notorious Girton conference,[39] also caused a stir among the members. He later wrote: 'Lake and I refused to make things easier for Liberals by showing connections between Synoptic germs and later Liberal concepts. We also refused to make things easier for the Sacramentalists. We were convinced that the present time is one in which the Church needs a plainer statement of the difficulties of modern Christianity, that it may realise where it stands.'[40]

It was, however, the distinctive christological positions, particularly those of Modernists such as Rashdall and Bethune-Baker, which gave the English Modernist movement prominence at this time, and was the source of bitter controversy. It appeared that these English Modernists rejected the miraculous in the Christian religion and so were blurring the fundamental distinction between God and man, Creator and creature. Following the Girton conference, Darwell Stone and others submitted a gravamen, and there was a debate in the Upper House of Convocation of Canterbury at which the traditional Nicene faith was affirmed. This controversy also led indirectly to the appointment of the Archbishops' Commission on Christian Doctrine.[41]

A brief comparison can now be made between the different approaches of Liberal Catholicism, Liberal Protestantism and English Modernism. This matter is complex: the terms 'Liberal' and

'Modernist' require careful definition because they can be given more than one meaning, and a scholar's biblical work and his dogmatic position may not always be clearly inter-related. The first area of difference was the value placed on the institutional Church. To the Liberal Catholic the concept of the Church was all-important, while many Liberal Protestants and Modernists disliked institutional ecclesiology. This is connected with an interpretation of the person of Christ, and raises the question of the relationship between the Christ worshipped in the Church and the Jesus of history. What was the link between what Jesus said and what was said about him? Was the institution of the Catholic Church, with its worship of a supernatural Christ, based on a mistake? The Liberal Catholic, especially when influenced by Catholic Modernism, maintained that the exalted Christ worshipped in the Church was the logical extension of the life and teaching of Jesus of Nazareth. Here the assessment of the New Testament records and the respective analyses of the theories of Paul, John and the synoptic evangelists were the essential factors. The Modernists, under Liberal Protestant influence, generally maintained that the moral, ethical and spiritual teachings of the earthly Jesus were what was vital. Here, however, the position was complicated by the eschatological interpretation of Jesus given by Loisy and Schweitzer. Also there was the question, uppermost at the time, of the value to be given to science and the evolutionary process, and hence of the relationship of Christianity to modern thought in general. Liberal Catholics, being on the whole doctrinally conservative, were opposed to the interpretation of Christianity in terms of evolution. As Hoskyns was to write later, 'The Lady Margaret Professor of Divinity [Dr Bethune-Baker] recently defined the immediate task of Christian theology to be the re-expression of the Christian faith in terms of evolution. I would venture to suggest that the task of the Christian theologian is rather to preserve the Christian Doctrine of God from the corrupting influence of the dogma of evolution, at least as that doctrine is popularly understood.'[42]

Finally reference must be made to the situation at the University of Cambridge, to which Hoskyns went as an undergraduate and where he was later to be a theological teacher from 1919 until his death in 1937. Writing of the religion at Cambridge at the time, V.H.H. Green comments: 'At Cambridge liberal or near modernist theology for long remained a dominant force; though Sir Edwyn Hoskyns, fellow of Corpus, who was much indebted to Karl Barth, reacting against its implicit Pelagianism, heralded the revival of biblical theology.'[43]

Presumably Green is referring here to W.R. Inge and J.F. Bethune-Baker, who were Lady Margaret Professors from 1907 to 1911 and from 1911 to 1934 respectively. Raven became Regius Professor in 1932, and maybe Green is describing them as 'liberal or near modernist', but it is doubtful if this approach could have dominated the whole theological school. However, the Cambridge theological school had already gained an international reputation from about 1860 onwards due to the work of the so-called 'Cambridge trio', J.B. Lightfoot, B.F. Westcott and F.J.A. Hort, their influence being mainly in the areas of textual criticism and ecclesiastical history. Lightfoot's work has been judged as 'stable and sturdy'[44] and infused with the characteristic English spirit of caution and sobriety, while Westcott, although as a theologian he had depth and imagination, was timid and conservative, being afraid to ask questions to which the answers might prove disturbing.[45] Hort was probably the most exact scholar of the three, but because of his own stringent requirements his corpus of published work was small. Despite the remarkable scholarship of the 'Cambridge trio', their work was well in the past by the early part of this century, but it did provide a solid foundation for continuing theological work.

H.B. Swete had succeeded Westcott as Regius Professor in 1890 and, although he was very learned, he was also shy, diffident, cautious and sober, and many felt that he was unfitted to succeed the great Dr Westcott. P. Gardner-Smith described how 'the days of King Edward VII were quiet times in Cambridge', and how he attended 'the placid lecture of Dr Swete from 12.10 to 1.00 p.m.' and that 'no more soothing experience could be imagined'; but the undergraduate 'knew nothing about foreign theology', and he is not sure if 'most of his lecturers knew very much more.'[46] An exception was F.C. Burkitt[47] who was certainly interested in foreign theology, for it was he who wrote a preface to introduce the English translations of Schweitzer's *The Quest of the Historical Jesus* (1910). Nevertheless Ramsey saw the period as memorable for the work of New Testament scholarship at Cambridge, with Armitage Robinson, Swete and Burkitt continuing the work of criticism and exegesis begun by the great 'Cambridge trio' in the 1860s.[48]

We have seen how the biblical theology of the first three decades of the twentieth century, especially within the Church of England, was closely linked to party affiliations. This theology was at the beginning of the period primarily historical, but biblical criticism was slowly taking root, and many scholars, including Hoskyns, were greatly interested in theological developments abroad. However, because English scholarship was insular by nature, these foreign developments took a long time to be used and understood in England.

NOTES

1. H.J. Rose, *A Letter to the Lord Bishop of London in reply to Mr Pusey's work on the causes of Rationalism in Germany*, London, 1829, p. 161, quoted by C.F. Evans in 'Queen or Cinderella', University of Durham, 1960, p. 6.

2. Hoskyns' admiration for Pusey can be illustrated from a reference in a letter to Karl Barth *Cambridge Sermons*, pp. 218–21. Hoskyns expresses gratitude that Pusey 'told the Church of England to set forth the meaning of the Holy Scripture itself, to "extract" truth from not to "import" truths into it' (p. 221).

3. S.C. Carpenter, *Church and People 1789–1889*, London, 1953, p. 537.

4. *Gore to Temple*, p. vii.

5. W.L. Knox and A.R. Vidler, *The Development of Modern Catholicism*, London, 1933, p. 114.

6. Ibid., p. 116.

7. Ibid., p. 123.

8. Gore was Vice-Principal of Cuddesdon in 1880–4 and later Principal of Pusey House, an establishment designed to further Pusey's aims and ideals. For further information on Gore, see J. Carpenter, *Gore: A Study in Liberal Catholic Thought*, London, 1960; A.M. Ramsey, *Charles Gore and Anglican Theology*, London, 1955; G.L. Prestige, *The Life of Charles Gore: A Great Englishman*, London, 1935; and A.R. Vidler, 'Bishop Gore and Liberal Catholicism', in *Essays in Liberality*, London, 1957, pp. 126–51.

9. C. Gore, ed., *Lux Mundi*, London, 1889, p. 360.

10. C.F. Evans, 'The Inspiration of the Bible' in *On the Authority of the Bible*, London, 1960, p. 27.

11. E.C. Hoskyns to Dr Albert Mansbridge, 30 May 1932, noted in Carpenter, op. cit., p. 104, note 33. Evidence of Gore's increased caution can be seen not only in his own contribution to *A New Commentary on Holy Scripture*, London, 1928, which he edited, but in the somewhat nervous footnotes which he added to the contributions of others.

12. For the meaning of the term 'Liberal Catholicism', see Carpenter, op. cit., pp. 42ff, and Vidler, op. cit., p. 129.

13. Catholic Modernism was a wide and diverse movement within the Roman Church generally relating to reform. It was especially powerful from 1880 until 1907–8 when it was forbidden by Papal legislation. This is a phenomenon to which constant reference will have to be made, especially to the biblical work of A.F. Loisy (1857–1940) and G. Tyrrell (1861–1909). Its

influence upon English biblical scholarship has not yet been fully discussed.

14. *Gore to Temple*, p. 108.
15. H.L. Stewart, *A Century of Anglo-Catholicism*, London, 1929, p. 215.
16. *Gore to Temple*, p. 109.
17. W.R. Matthews, *The Green Quarterly*, April 1933, p. 71, quoted, *Modernist Movement*, p. 251, note 1.
18. Knox and Vidler, op. cit., p. 270.
19. *Gore to Temple*, pp. 94f.
20. The name 'Liberal Protestant' is usually given to those who support the views of the school linked with Adolf von Harnack (1851–1930), see Chapter 2.2, note 33. Broadly, Liberal Protestants maintain that Jesus' teachings were centred around the Fatherhood of God and the brotherhood of man, and that the Catholic Church had obscured this basic message and allowed alien Hellenistic influences to intrude into Christian theology; what was now needed was that this 'husk' must be shed so that the real 'kernel' could be reached.
21. L.E. Elliott-Binns, *Religion in the Victorian Era*, 2nd edn, London, 1946.
22. *Gore to Temple*, p. 66; *Modernist Movement*, p. 247.
23. *20th Century Defenders*, an appended note on Anglican Modern Churchmanship, pp. 123f.
24. W.R. Inge, *Outspoken Essays*, 1st series, London, 1919, ch. 6, pp. 137–171.
25. P. Gardner, *Modernism in the English Church*, London, 1926, p. 173.
26. See also *D.N.B. 1912–21*, Oxford, 1927, pp. 482–4, by G. Turner; and W. Lock, *J.T.S.*, XXII, 1921, pp. 97–104, with bibliography of published works by A. Souter, pp. 193–205.
27. W. Sanday, *Bishop Gore's Challenge to Criticism*, London, 1914.
28. W. Sanday, *The Life of Christ in Recent Research*, Oxford, 1907, p. 88.
29. *Gore to Temple*, Appendix A: 'The Influence of Albert Schweitzer', pp. 171–4.
30. See *Dictionary of National Biography* (hereafter 'D.N.B.') *1931–1940*, Oxford, 1949, pp. 836–8, by L.W. Grensted.
31. B.H. Streeter, *The Four Gospels: A Study of Origins*, London, 1924, p. 318.
32. Streeter's Proto-Luke theory has not gained wide agreement; a later commentator on Luke, J.M. Creed, felt that there was little to be said for the theory and dismissed it in a footnote: see J.M. Creed, *The Gospel according to St. Luke*, London, 1930, p. viii, note 1.
33. S. Neill, *The Interpretation of the New Testament 1861–1961*, paperback edn, Oxford, 1966, p. 122.
34. See *D.N.B. 1951–1960*, Oxford 1971, pp. 529–32, by W.R. Matthews.
35. W.R. Inge, 'The Theology of the Fourth Gospel', in H.B. Swete, ed., *Cambridge Biblical Essays*, Cambridge, 1909, p. 258.
36. See *D.N.B. 1941–1950*, Oxford, 1959, pp. 466–7, by C.F. Grant. Also

R.P. Casey, S. Lake, A.K. Lake, eds, *Quantulacumque: Studies presented to Kirsopp Lake by pupils, colleagues and friends*, London, 1937, with biographical note by his son Gerard Kirsopp Lake, pp. vii f.

37. See *D.N.B. 1941–1950*, pp. 426f., by P. Gardner-Smith.

38. *Gore to Temple*, p. 70.

39. The Girton Conference was held at Girton College, Cambridge, in August 1921 as the annual conference of the Modern Churchmen's Union. Some 'notorious' christological statements were made apparently denying the Virgin Birth, the miraculous and the bodily resurrection of Christ, and a bitter controversy arose after these matters were highlighted by the press. The report of the conference, entitled 'Christ and Creeds', is to be found in *The Modern Churchman*, XI, 1921. Hoskyns was present at the conference, A.M.G. Stephenson, 'Girton 1921', *The Modern Churchman*, XI, 1967–8, p. 11.

40. *Gore to Temple*, p. 70.

41. *20th Century Defenders*, p. 123.

42. *Cambridge Sermons*, p. 35.

43. V.H.H. Green, *Religion at Oxford and Cambridge*, London, 1964, p. 344.

44. O. Chadwick, *The Victorian Church*, Part II, 2nd edn, Cambridge, 1972, p. 70.

45. B.M.G. Reardon, *From Coleridge to Gore*, London, 1971, p. 351; Neill, op. cit., p. 89.

46. P. Gardner Smith, 'The Last Fifty Years of Cambridge Theology', *The Cambridge Review*, 9 October, 1954, p. 26.

47. F.C. Burkitt (1864–1935) was Norrisian Professor at Cambridge, 1905–35, and therefore was a colleague of Hoskyns during most of his time at Cambridge. Burkitt had a brilliant and unconventional mind, doing much work on the Syriac versions of the New Testament and on Syriac liturgies. He was a champion of the eschatological, apocalyptic interpretation of Jesus and was influenced by Albert Schweitzer: see also articles by E.C. Ratcliff, *J.T.S.*, XXXVI, 1935, pp. 225–53, and by J.F. Bethune-Baker in *D.N.B. 1931–1940*, pp. 124f.

48. *Gore to Temple*, p. 130.

2.1

EARLY LIBERAL CATHOLICISM

The circumstances of religious and theological controversy in the early decades of the twentieth century in Britain, which have been sketched in the previous chapter, are important for an understanding of at least one element in Hoskyns' development as a biblical theologian. He had been born in 1884 in the vicarage of St Clement's Notting Hill, where his father, later to be Bishop and Rector of Burnley and finally Bishop of Southwell, had been the incumbent since 1881; and he had grown up in a 'tradition of sober, upright, slightly austere High Church Anglicanism'.[1] After school at Haileybury, he went to his father's old college, Jesus, Cambridge, where he graduated with a second class in Part II of the historical tripos in 1906. After a period of study in Berlin undertaken on the advice of F.J. Foakes-Jackson, the Dean of the college, he went to Wells Theological College and in 1908 was ordained to a title at St Ignatius' Sunderland, a notable parish in the Anglo-Catholic tradition. What Hoskyns thought of that tradition at the time can be seen from a lecture he delivered in German at the University of Tübingen on the Oxford Movement. J.O. Cobham gives good grounds for believing that it was given while Hoskyns was still a curate at St Ignatius': 'It had changed our churches from auditoriums for a preacher into houses of prayer. It had recovered Holy Communion as the centre of the religious life of the Church. It had, as a later development, introduced ritualism as a useful means towards the winning of the common people. It had given us open churches, instead of churches that were locked from one Sunday to the next. It had put clergy under discipline. It had recovered the observance of the Church's year. It had introduced Gothic architecture. Without separating Church and State, it had ensured the independence of the Church from the State.'[2]

In 1912 Hoskyns was appointed Warden of Stephenson Hall, the Church hostel in the University of Sheffield, and during the First World War served as chaplain to the forces, won the Military Cross and was mentioned in despatches. It was during the war, in 1916, that he was appointed a Fellow of Corpus Christi College, Cambridge, and College Lecturer in Divinity, though given leave of absence until the end of the war. Hence he did not take up his duties there till 1919, when he was also appointed Dean of Chapel, a post he held until his death in 1937.

The college which he had joined was already a long way on in a transformation from the centre of Evangelicalism which it had been in the nineteenth century to being a home of the liberal Anglo-Catholic tradition.[3] The transformation had begun under R.T. Caldwell, who became Master in 1906 and was responsible for the appointment as director of studies in Natural Science of Will Spens; Spens was to gain a reputation as a lay Anglo-Catholic theologian especially through his book *Belief and Practice* (1915), and later became a member of the Archbishops' Commission on Christian Doctrine. E.G. Selwyn, also an Anglo-Catholic, was appointed as Lecturer in Classics and was to be the founder of the journal *Theology* (1920) and the editor of *Essays Catholic and Critical* (1926). This policy was continued by Caldwell's successor as Master, E.C. Pearce, who as Dean of Chapel had 'played an important part in modifying the chapel services and initiating the move to make its teaching representative of Liberal Anglo-Catholic theology.'[4] On his departure in 1927 to be Bishop of Derby, Pearce was succeeded as Master by Spens, as he had been succeeded as Dean of Chapel by Hoskyns.[5]

Thus as a result of his upbringing, his first and only experience of the parochial ministry and his membership of Corpus Christi College, Hoskyns stood within the Anglo-Catholic tradition. C.H. Smyth describes him as a 'staunch Anglo-Catholic', adding that he 'was never in any danger of becoming in any narrow sense a "party" man, or of making what Bishop Creighton, with unerring judgement, regarded as the supreme mistake of Laud's career — the mistake of fighting for great principles on small issues.'[6] Some of his earliest utterances and writings came from within, and were at the service of, that tradition — the booklet *Christ and Catholicism*, produced for the 1923 Anglo-Catholic Congress, and two addresses — one, 'The Eucharist in the New Testament', delivered at the 1927 Anglo-Catholic Congress and the other, 'The Apostolicity of the Church', delivered at the Congress of 1930.

Christ and Catholicism was one of the fifty-two booklets prepared for the 1923 Congress, some of which were written by first-rate scholars, either of that time or of the future as, for example, *The Deity of Christ* (no. 4) by N.P. Williams; *Is there a true religion?* (no. 2) by K.E. Kirk; *The Christian Moral Ideal* (no. 20) by E.J. Bicknell, and *The Old and New Testaments* (nos. 17 and 18) also by E.J. Bicknell. Although it consisted of barely twenty pages, it is 'of interest as containing in germ much of his later thought'.[7] Its thesis was that Catholic Christianity can be traced back to the teaching of Christ, and that the Liberal Protestant notion of a 'simple' Gospel 'free of dogmas, free of the miraculous "supernatural" additions to genuine Christianity, free of sacramental and sacrificial worship, free of the Church'[8] must be seriously questioned. Its intention was to show that the New Testament and the Catholic Faith are not two different systems but vitally related to each other, and its method was to show that the Gospel of St John, written at the end of the first century, was a legitimate development in the Christian tradition from the earlier Gospel of St Mark; 'a comparison of these two gospels ought to reveal the main lines of development within primitive Christianity, and to enable us to judge how far this development was due to a legitimate or illegitimate interpretation of the Gospel of Jesus.'[9] For St John the community of the true worshippers of God was unique because it had been brought into being by the only begotten Son of God and so possessed an unbroken contact with him, so that 'St John's narrative is not the record of the corruption of a simple teaching; it is an explanation of the supernatural origin of a simple experience. St John's gospel, therefore, presumed that the Christianity of his day was ecclesiastical, sacramental, and sacrificial, and that it claimed a definitely supernatural origin.'[10] In St Mark's Gospel, however, Christ is depicted as performing the Messianic acts of riding into Jerusalem and cleansing the Temple in order to fulfil prophecy. These events, and the violent Jewish reaction to them, are only intelligible if it is assumed that Christ openly and publicly claimed to be the Messiah of Jewish prophecy. But the Messiah must suffer and be crucified, so renouncing 'the idea of the Messianic Kingdom as a Jewish state ruled by an earthly King'.[11] This mystery of Christ's life and death is to be extended also to his disciples who followed him; the mission to the world is placed in their hands and they are to share in his humiliation, as they continue his ministry. By Christ's sacrifice made once for all, the new Covenant was brought into being, and it was given a new rite of sacrificial worship in the sharing of Christ's Body and Blood in the Eucharist. This new covenant and worship must be accompanied by 'the righteousness of the heart and the true love and knowledge of God'.[12] Thus 'the primitive Christians did not corrupt his teaching; rather, in the light of their experience, they learnt to understand it. Our Lord made supernatural claims not only for his own person, but also for the community which he consciously brought into being.'[13] Christ therefore taught a Catholic religion, involving membership in a visible community possessing supernatural powers, with a ministry and sacrificial worship 'by which was mediated

the righteousness of the heart and love of the brethren.'[14] Catholics can
confidently claim a biblical basis for their faith, and the assurance that
'Catholicism is not the outcome of a gradual corruption of the primitive
Christian Gospel, but is rather a legitimate interpretation of the life and
teaching of our Lord himself.'[15]

Although *Christ and Catholicism* reads like any Anglo-Catholic mani-
festo and has the corresponding limitations in that it requires a more
detailed and careful mapping of the line from Mark to John to Catholicism than was actually given, it already illustrates a basic and characteristic tenet of Hoskyns, namely that there was a genuine continuity
between Christ and Catholicism, and that the Catholic faith is not a
corruption of Christ's original thought. In this he was sharing in some
measure the position of Catholic Modernism as it had been worked out
by Loisy in *L'Évangile et l'Église* (1902), while conversely the
Liberal Protestant position, that Christ taught a 'simple' religion of the
love of God and the love of man, was called into question. This latter
position was shown to be open to criticism on scholarly grounds,
although in his attack Hoskyns did not employ the radical criticism used
by Loisy and he mentions no particular scholars by name.

One particular aspect of the general thesis of *Christ and Catholicism*
was the overall subject of the Anglo-Catholic Congress of 1927 — the
sacraments. This must be set within the controversies that were raging
at the time. It was the link between Jesus and the Church, with its
supernatural sacramental life, which was denied by the Modernists.
Hence Hoskyns concludes: 'Our controversy with the Bishop of Birmingham[16] and with those whom he represents does not concern
primarily the Eucharist, but the Gospel. . . . In this particular controversy it must in any case be stated, and stated quite clearly, that we
Catholics have the New Testament wholly on our side.'[17] Hoskyns
maintained that as the 'Catholic Religion is the relation of the power
and the wisdom and the love of God in a living organism of flesh and
blood,'[18] so the question must be asked as to how the Catholic religion is
related to the religion of the New Testament and in particular how its
worship is related to the worship of the Apostolic Church and to the
teaching of Christ. Here again Hoskyns adopted Loisy's position,[19]
namely that a fully developed liturgy cannot be expected to be found in
the Apostolic Church, but that Catholic worship is a legitimate development of Apostolic Christianity and so 'we ought to be able to discover in
the earliest Christian writings signs of an adjustment of worship so that
the Gospel may be thereby expressed in concrete form.'[20] Hoskyns

continued with a consideration of the Gospel of St John, for whom the whole activity of the Christian Church is to be found in the manifestation of the incarnate and the crucified Son of God for the salvation of the world. Consequently, he defines Christian worship 'as eating the Flesh of the Son of Man and drinking his Blood'.[21] Johannine eucharistic theology is therefore based upon the Incarnation of the Son of God and upon his death on the cross as a sacrifice for sin. The language of John 6 (vv. 53 and 54 are quoted) was not an adjustment of the Gospel to Hellenistic sacramental mania but the opposite; 'it is the completion of the first stage of adjusting Christian worship to the Gospel.'[22] The same process of adjustment was provided by Paul in 1 Cor. 11 for the purpose of preserving the rite from abuse.

Two questions are then asked: How is this Johannine-Pauline adjustment of Christian worship to the Gospel related to our Lord's words and actions at the Last Supper? And how is it related to the worship of the primitive Church in Jerusalem?[23] The first question is referred back to St Mark's narrative of the institution of the Last Supper which was eschatological in form and structure. As to the second, little evidence can be found of the nature of the pre-Pauline Apostolic worship in Jerusalem, since St Luke did not precisely explain what he meant by the expression 'the breaking of the bread', but 'whatever conclusion we may tentatively accept as to the significance of St Luke's language, it seems abundantly clear that the line St Paul — St John — Catholic worship is one line, and that it finds its adequate explanation and origin only in our Lord's death and in his words and actions at the Last Supper taken together as forming one sacrificial act.'[24] In this short paper, the thesis is reiterated that the Catholic mode of eucharistic theology and worship is a legitimate development from early Christianity and that it contained within itself the vital elements of the original eschatological Gospel of Christ. Catholics can take comfort from the fact that their religion is biblically based and that their opponents have missed the point of Catholicism, not because of any inherent weakness in the Catholic system, but because of their own lack of objective judgement.

Hoskyns' contribution to the 1930 Anglo-Catholic Congress was on 'The Apostolicity of the Church', and as the title suggests it deals with the concepts of Church and Apostle. Here, although he still speaks of the continuity of the Church with the Gospel, he emphasises in addition (and the importance of this will become increasingly evident) the necessary subjection of the Church to the Gospel. The idea of the Church was derived from the Old Testament concept of the Hebrew people as the chosen people of God, which in the Christian Church constitutes the new people of God who 'obeyed the Messianic call to repentance and gathered round Jesus the Messiah'.[25] During the earthly ministry of Jesus his disciples were only potentially the Church of God, emerging after his resurrection as the nucleus of the redeemed community with the call to declare their message courageously and openly to the world. Although the word 'Church' only occurs twice in the Gospels (Matt.16:18, 18:17), the idea of the Church as the new people of God is found throughout the New Testament, as an expression of the messiahship of Jesus and of the essence of the Gospel. 'Thus understood, the Apostolicity of the Church is entirely secure on the basis of a most rigorously scientific and critical study of the Gospels.'[26] Hoskyns then deals briefly with eschatology, the Evangelical insistence on eschatology being seen as entirely necessary in this messianic context. He maintains that the teaching of Jesus was not merely concerned with the heralding of the imminent end of this world (presumably this was a criticism of Schweitzer's approach, although he is not mentioned by name), but with the urgent demands of the present and the consequent act of doing the will of God at once and without delay. The Church's mission 'is concerned only to follow the Lord in declaring effectively that human destiny depends upon its acceptance or rejection of the Son of God.'[27] The apostolicity of the Church is not undermined by the length of its existence in history, since the significance of the work of the Church is declared by the eschatology of the Gospels.

The work of bishops is then related to the ministry of the original Apostles, who had seen the Lord and who were thereby enabled to bear witness to his life, death and resurrection. The bishops were to preserve in each local Church the witness of the Apostles, the history of the episcopate being not merely a matter of ecclesiastical organisation (as maintained by Streeter) but 'to explain how the Church was enabled to preserve the teaching of the Apostles of the Lord at a time when the personal links with the Jesus of history, with the Flesh and Blood of Christ, were broken by death and by martyrdom.'[28] Finally Hoskyns refers to the controversies of his own time. Therefore Catholics are not primarily concerned here with organisation, but with the nature of the Gospel: 'Taught by the New Testament, we are bound to think of the Episcopate as preserving the witness of the Apostles, and to demand this of the bishops. The bishops are not mystical persons to whom we owe some strange kind of undefined mysterious obedience. The bishops are responsible to bear witness to Jesus Christ, the Son of God, and to hold

the Church to that witness. Nor does the Episcopate offer an oppor-
tunity to gifted individuals to occupy an exalted position and to
tyrannize over those who are endowed to a lesser degree with intellectual
or other gifts.'[29]

Perhaps there is another allusion here to Bishop Barnes of
Birmingham (see note 16), but whatever the specific reference, a major
theological point emerges: that the authority of bishops depends solely
on their link with the Apostles (although in this paper Hoskyns does not
define Apostolic succession) and on their witness to Jesus Christ.

These three short pieces are to be seen in the context of addresses to
Anglican Catholic gatherings comprising priests and laity, those who
had received scholarly training and those who had not; but, given that
context, they represented a considerable achievement. First, their thesis
that Catholicism is based upon, and represents, a legitimate development
of Jesus was presented in an arresting style and in a manner both
scholarly and attentive to current issues. While this presentation owed
much to Catholic Modernism, especially that of Loisy, there was already
a hint in the paper on Apostolicity that the Church must be constantly
tested by the Bible, an idea which was increasingly to dominate
Hoskyns' thought, as when he maintains that the Church 'is an
organism which needs perpetual Biblical control.'[30] Secondly, though
non-technical, it was these pieces, along with the writings of others of
the same time, which gave the Anglo-Catholic movement in the 1920s
and 1930s its credibility. They showed that the movement was not one
of irrational emotionalism or of superstition, especially towards the
sacraments, but that it was based on sound biblical and historical principles. Catholic doctrine of the Eucharist, for example, was based on the
'correct' interpretation of John 6 and its development from Christ's
institution of the Last Supper. Thirdly, the pieces assisted in the
continuing battle of Anglo-Catholics with the English Modernist movement and the theological liberalism which was still influential both in
university and parish life, and constituted a step in that direction which
was later to be described by admirers as having delivered us from 'the
tyranny of that Liberal Humanitarianism in which old-fashioned agnosticism had naturally tended to take refuge',[31] or as 'the victory of a
constructive Liberal Catholicism that was Evangelical in its very essence
over the popularized Liberal-Protestant interpretation of the Gospels.'[32]

NOTES

1. Neill, op. cit., p. 212.

2. Cobham, op. cit., pp. 287f.

3. For details see P. Bury, *The College of Corpus Christi and the Blessed Virgin Mary: A History from 1822–1952*, Cambridge, 1952, pp. 119ff. Note also the remarks of M. Cowling, *Religion and Public Doctrine in Modern England*, Cambridge, 1980, p. 73, and of T.E.B. Howarth, *Cambridge Between Two Wars*, London, 1978, p. 165.

4. Bury, op. cit., p. 137.

5. ibid., pp. 251f. Bury maintains that Hoskyns made his own mark in the College 'as a notable Director of Theological Studies and as a University lecturer whose special subjects were New Testament theology and ethics. His influence here, following upon that already exercised in Corpus by Mr E.G. Selwyn, the Master Dr Pearce and Mr Will Spens, went far to justify a remark made by Canon B.H. Streeter that Corpus had become the only College in either university which, during the last twenty-four years, had not only known how to teach theology, but had built up a theological school.'

6. *Cambridge Sermons*, pp. xi f.

7. C.H. Smyth, 'In Memoriam: Canon Sir Edwyn Hoskyns, 1884–1937', *Theology*, XXXV, 1937, p. 137.

8. E.C. Hoskyns, *Christ and Catholicism*, Anglo-Catholic Congress Books, 12, 1923, p. 2.

9. ibid., p. 3.

10. ibid., pp. 7f.

11. ibid., p. 11.

12. ibid., p. 18.

13. ibid., pp. 19f.

14. ibid., p. 20.

15. ibid.

16. *D.N.B. 1951–1960*, Oxford, 1971, article on E.W. Barnes by A.E.J. Rawlinson, pp. 65–7. Barnes was Bishop of Birmingham (1924–53) and as a broad churchman 'showed himself negatively hostile towards all forms of the doctrine of the Real Presence of Christ in the Eucharist . . . The essence of Christianity, as he understood it and as he practised it, was to be found in the personal discipleship of the Jesus of the Gospels, and in the acceptance of an ethic based on the Sermon on the Mount' (p. 65). 'In 1925 trouble threatened by reason of his refusal to institute a patron's nominee to a vacant benefice unless he agreed in advance to discontinue the practice of reservation which had been customary in the parish' (p. 66). This was the beginning of many similar incidents of this kind and of the legal battles which accompanied them. The controversy was bitter and opinion divided. E.G. Selwyn wrote of Barnes, '. . . . scornful and cruel,

the Bishop has shown himself not a shepherd but a wolf; and men cannot
but feel they will be betraying Christ if they yield to his rule' (editorial,
Theology, XV, 1927, p. 277). However, H.J.A. Major praised Barnes'
'firm administrative methods and his trenchant criticism of sacramental
superstitions' (editorial, *The Modern Churchman*, XVII, 1927–8, p. 508).
For a modern estimate of Barnes see A.R. Vidler, 'Bishop Barnes: A
Centenary Retrospect', *The Modern Churchman*, XVIII, 1974–5,
pp. 87–98. J. Barnes's biography of his father, *Ahead of his Age: Bishop
Barnes of Birmingham*, London, 1979, ought to be read alongside A.R.
Vidler's review of the same, *Theology*, LXXXIII, 1980, pp. 302–4.

17. E.C. Hoskyns, 'The Eucharist in the New Testament', Report of the
    Anglo-Catholic Congress, London, 1927, p. 56.
18. ibid., p. 51.
19. A.F. Loisy, *L'Évangile et l'Église*, Paris, 1902; Eng. transl. *The
    Gospel and the Church*, London, 1908, especially section VI on Christian
    Worship, pp. 226–77. For example, 'The starting point of the system is,
    as has been indicated, the baptism of Jesus and the Last Supper. The end is
    still to come, as sacramental development continuing to follow the same
    general lines, can only end with the Church herself' (p. 249).
20. 'The Eucharist in the New Testament', p. 51.
21. ibid., p. 52.
22. ibid., p. 53.
23. ibid., p. 54.
24. ibid., p. 56.
25. E.C. Hoskyns, 'The Apostolicity of the Church', Report of the Anglo-
    Catholic Congress, London, 1930, p. 86.
26. ibid., p. 87.
27. ibid., p. 88.
28. ibid., p. 89.
29. ibid., p. 90.
30. E.C. Hoskyns, *We are the Pharisees* . . ., London, 1960, p. 61.
31. *Cambridge Sermons*, p. viii.
32. ibid., p. ix.

2.2

CONTACTS WITH GERMAN THEOLOGY AND THEOLOGIANS

It may thus be seen that Hoskyns' theology was deeply rooted in the Church and in membership of the Church. This, however, was not its only root. Another was German theology, especially German New Testament theology, with which he was intimately acquainted. His Anglo-Catholic addresses made no reference to individual scholars, and could hardly have done so, but they nevertheless reflect a scholarly background. As has been noted above, Hoskyns, on the advice of the Dean of his College, had gone immediately after taking the historical tripos to the University of Berlin to study under Adolf Harnack,[33] and during his curacy at Sunderland he gave lectures in German at the University of Tübingen, one on the Oxford Movement, which was chiefly concerned with the Church, and the other on George Tyrrell's *Christianity at the Cross Roads*, which was concerned with the cut and thrust of scholarly debate on the New Testament both in Germany and elsewhere in reaction to Harnack's position.

Hoskyns, as was plain, had been strongly influenced by Harnack and acknowledged his debt to him. 'For a whole year I sat under him in Berlin and owe more to him than perhaps anyone else. Never before had one realised the greatness of our Lord's character than when Harnack talked of him. No one could speak of our Lord with more reverence and personal devotion than he did. And again, Harnack taught one to try and think things out for oneself. Cambridge never taught one that.'[34] In the winter of 1899–1900 Harnack had delivered extempore lectures to classes of some 600 drawn from all the faculties in the University of Berlin. An enthusiastic listener took them down in shorthand and they were subsequently published under the title *Das Wesen des Christentums*.[35] This publication was an 'instant and unprecedented success',[36] and showed that Liberal Protestantism 'had reached the apex of its development and the peak of its popularity'.[37] Harnack attempted to reduce Christianity to its original essence and in so doing outlined the essence of Christianity as he saw it, tried to discover the true significance of the person of Jesus, and maintained that ecclesiastical Christianity was a corruption of the original Gospel. For Harnack the message of Jesus was 'Firstly the Kingdom of God and its coming. Secondly God the Father and the infinite value of the human soul. Thirdly the higher righteousness and the commandment of love. That Jesus' message is so great and so powerful lies in the fact that it is so simple and on the other hand so rich; so simple as to be exhausted in each of the leading thoughts which he uttered, so rich that every one of these thoughts seems to be inexhaustible and the full meaning of the sayings and parables beyond our reach.'[38] Naturally Jesus came into conflict with the official leaders of Judaism because they 'thought of God as of a despot guarding the ceremonial observances in His Household; he breathed in the presence of God . . . They had made this religion into an earthly trade, and there was nothing more detestable; he proclaimed the living God and the soul's nobility.'[39] For Harnack, therefore, the Gospel is the declaration of the spiritual liberty of mankind, and it is this sense of liberation which runs through the whole of his exposition of Christianity.

But what is the essence of Christianity for Harnack? It is concerned with the fatherhood of God and the brotherhood of man, and it is in this context that Harnack used his famous analogy of the kernel and the husk in distinguishing what is traditional and what is peculiar in Jesus' message. The kernel of the message is 'the kingdom of God' which 'comes by coming to the individual, by entering into his soul and laying hold of it'.[40] Harnack believed that the Kingdom has a triple meaning: it is supernatural and not a product of ordinary life; it is a religious blessing which formed an inner link with the living God; and it is the most important experience that a person can have, that on which everything else depended.[41] Harnack's view of the Kingdom was that when its other-worldly aspect was removed like the husk of a nut, then Jesus' true intention would be known, namely that the Kingdom was to be found in the heart of the believer. This process would also give Jesus his proper significance as a teacher of the brotherhood of man. Jesus was convinced that he was the Son of God, because he knew God in a way which no one had ever known God before; this premise was based on Matt. 11:25–27 and Luke 10:21–22 (Matt. 11:27 is quoted). The consciousness which Jesus possessed as Son of God was 'nothing but the practical consequences of knowing God as the Father and as his Father. Rightly understood, the name of Son means nothing but the knowledge of God.'[42] Jesus then directed the attention of humankind to the promise of God's grace and mercy; he demanded that individuals should decide between God or Mammon, an eternal or an earthly life, of humility or self-righteousness. The individual 'is called upon to listen to the glad message of mercy and the Fatherhood of God, and to make up his mind whether he will be on God's side and the Eternal's, or on the side of the world and of time. The Gospel, as Jesus proclaimed it, has to do with the Father only and not with the Son.'[43]

Yet with the passage of time, this 'simple' message of what originally Christianity was meant to be about had been transformed and corrupted by Catholicism; this is because the Catholic Church in both its Eastern and its Western forms is a betrayal of the Gospel, since it identifies faith with a doctrine, and the community of believers with a hierarchically-controlled organisation. The whole outward and visible institution of a Church claiming divine dignity has no foundation whatever in the Gospel. Protestantism, by contrast, is a return to Christianity as it was originally meant to be, and although Harnack warned Protestants of the threats that faced them, nevertheless 'Protestantism reckons — this is the solution — upon the Gospel being something so simple, so divine, and therefore so truly human, as to be most certain of being understood when it is left entirely free, and also as to produce essentially the same experiences and convictions in individual souls.'[44] Although Luther's reformation struck a great blow in the cause of spiritual liberty, yet the time had now arrived for another reformation. Unfortunately Luther had no means of distinguishing between kernel and husk, original deposit and alien growth, and hence scholasticism had remained in the ascendant in Protestant orthodoxy. What was now needed, according to Harnack, was a return to the liberty of the Gospel in all its simplicity and vital humanity.

Naturally many voices were raised for and against Harnack's position. Hoskyns admitted that Harnack wrote purely as a historian; he did not write apologies for Christianity. Rather, 'he has set himself the task of finding the historic Jesus, what he was and what he taught. Harnack claims to have found him.'[45] The result of this historical search was that he could 'separate the person of our Lord from the Gospel . . . and finds almost at once this pure Gospel is perverted everywhere. As soon as he begins to study church history he finds a "growing catholicism" springing up everywhere, centering round sacraments, a priesthood with superhuman powers, a visible church, and in the centre of all the person of Christ, ascended, sitting on the right hand of power and himself — God. This catholicism grows worse and worse as the centuries go on. But such is the power of the Gospel that even in spite of this mass of thistles which grow up around it, it managed to shine through . . . till now at last we have got back to the historic Jesus, and see him as he was, unspoilt by catholicism — rescued by the liberal protestant critical school of modern Germany.'[46] But Hoskyns' major criticism here was that Harnack and his school could not 'explain how their Gospel of the love of God and your neighbour preached by a great prophet became a sacramental mystical religion centring round their prophet of God. . . . They will talk still about "growing catholicism" without giving the vaguest explanation how or why it should grow. This glaring defect in the Liberal Protestant position could not long be left unattacked.'[47]

One such attack had been made already in 1902 by the Catholic Modernist A.F. Loisy[48] in his *L'Évangile et l'Église*.[49] The book had a twofold purpose: to show that Harnack's Liberal Protestant version of Christianity was historically untrue on critical grounds, and hence spiritually unsatisfactory; and as a modernised apology for Catholicism to win approval among Catholics. Loisy was critical of Harnack for constructing his thesis on such a small number of texts, in fact only two major passages: Matt. 11:27, concerning the relation of Father and Son, and Luke 17:21, 'The Kingdom of God is within you.' Loisy complained that 'to build a general theory of Christianity on a small number of texts of moderate authority, neglecting the mass of incontestable texts of clear significance, would be to sin against the most elementary principles of criticism . . . Herr Harnack has not avoided this danger.'[50] Harnack's position was based on an unhistorical assumption that the essence of the Gospel consisted only in filial trust in God the Father; the selection of this single idea was the result of prejudice and must be examined. In reply Loisy argued that no rigid line should be drawn between Jesus and primitive Christianity, because 'we know Christ only by the tradition, across the tradition and in the tradition of the primitive Christians. . . . The attempt to define the essence of Christianity according to the pure Gospel of Jesus, apart from tradition, cannot succeed, for the mere idea of the Gospel without tradition is in flagrant contradiction with the facts submitted to criticism.'[51]

Loisy was equally critical of Harnack's interpretation of the Kingdom of God as interior and spiritual, maintaining that the Kingdom of God as preached by Jesus was thoroughly eschatological and dominated by apocalyptic conceptions, the idea of the celestial Kingdom being 'nothing but a great hope, and it is in this hope or nowhere that the historian should set the essence of the Gospel, as no other idea holds so prominent and so large a place in the teaching of Jesus.'[52] Loisy was critical, too, of Harnack's analogy of the kernel and the husk, the husk being the eschatological idea of the Kingdom, while the kernel was the individual's faith in the merciful God. For him these elements are 'intertwined, inseparable, essential'.[53] The Kingdom of God was not able to be seen as a gradual evolutionary process, and thus modernized; 'it cannot be too often repeated that Jesus only announced it in the Kingdom about to come, and he did not represent it as a work of slow progress.'[54] The faith of the early disciples took shape within the idea of the reign of God, the conception of God the Father being only one element which assisted in the general development of Christianity.

So also with Harnack's view about the divine sonship of Christ. The idea that Jesus knew God as none before had known him was based on a single text (Matt.11:27), and that text was 'a product of the Christian tradition of the earlier times'.[55] Both friends and enemies of Jesus identified him as Messiah, although Jesus in the course of his preaching did not announce this. Jesus' messianic office, like the preaching of the Kingdom, was eschatological, as in 'one sense Jesus was the Messiah, in another sense He was presently to become the Messiah.'[56]

As the messiahship of Jesus formed an integral part of the original Gospel, so the Church was indispensable for the preservation of the Gospel; Loisy therefore argued against Harnack that, far from being the corruption of the Gospel, the Church had maintained the life of the Gospel. 'Thus to reproach the Catholic Church for the development of the constitution is to reproach her for having chosen to live, and that, moreover, when her life was indispensable for the preservation of the Gospel itself. There is nowhere in her history any gap of continuity, or the absolute creation of a new system.'[57] What is more, the Church contains the basic elements of the original Gospel: the idea of an eschatological heavenly Kingdom, a Messiah who is the sole mediator of the Kingdom, and the idea of the apostolate which continues the work of the Messiah for future generations. Yet, while the Church preserved the original Gospel, she developed in her own way; so naturally the Church of the future is not precisely identical with the Church of the Apostles. 'To be identical with the religion of Jesus, it has no more need to reproduce exactly the forms of the Galilean Gospel than a man has need to preserve at fifty the proportions, features and manner of life of the day of his birth in order to be the same individual. The identity of a man is not ensured by making him return to his cradle.'[58] Christian dogma developed also along similar lines, because this was the attempt to give a reasonable account of, and to formulate the facts of, Christian experience. Hence, 'dogmas are not truths fallen from heaven and preserved by religious tradition in the precise form in which they first appeared. The historian sees in them the interpretation of religious facts, acquired by a laborious effort of theological thought. Although the dogmas may be Divine in origin and substance they are human in structure and composition.'[59]

Certainly Loisy submitted Harnack's position to a damaging if not fatal criticism, this being done by the use of pure argument rather than with abuse, so that 'the unbiased student can hardly deny that his refutation of them [Harnack and Sabatier] was successful and even prophetic.'[60] The popularity of Harnack's Liberal Protestantism waned steadily in Germany itself, where however it was Weiss and Schweitzer rather than Loisy who were regarded as having established the eschatological interpretation of the original Gospel. Thus W.G. Kümmel believes that Loisy's work 'was done in knowledge of, even if not in dependence on, the thought of Johannes Weiss,'[61] whereas A.R. Vidler had taken the opposite view: 'It is obviously difficult for German Protestants to believe that they have anything to learn from a French Roman Catholic.'[62]

Where did Hoskyns stand in this? The matter is somewhat complex, and Hoskyns was later to become involved in some debate about it.[63] On the one hand it came to be maintained later that Hoskyns 'found through Loisy an approach to the New Testament'.[64] We have already drawn attention to the basis for such a judgement in Hoskyns' earliest production. On the other hand, Vidler came to criticise Hoskyns precisely for overlooking Loisy's part in establishing the eschatological emphasis in the Gospels. He complained, referring to Hoskyns' later essay in *Essays Catholic and Critical*, that he 'appears to give all credit to J. Weiss and Schweitzer and to ignore Loisy entirely. The same writer, when referring to Catholic Modernism in general and to *L'Évangile et l'Église* in particular, likewise overlooks the importance of Loisy's work as an historic criticism of liberal Protestantism.'[67] To this Hoskyns was to reply in a private letter: 'On the whole, I think your rebuke unnecessarily hard. I was not concerned with the history of the recognition of eschatology in the Gospels, or with giving "credit"; but simply with the fact that it was Weiss and Schweitzer who introduced the tension of eschatology in technical New Testament work for most of us. We ought perhaps to have got it from Loisy, but we did not.'[68] Hoskyns' letter went on to note that Loisy's approach removed some of the acute pain for those who combined Catholic faith with New Testament criticism, and he expressed himself publicly in no uncertain terms on the official attitude of the Roman Church towards biblical criticism which had led to Loisy's excommunication: 'The Vatican has almost killed Biblical criticism in the Roman Church, and our Protestant Fundamentalists join hands with the Vatican in an attempt to name the critical study of the Bible blasphemous. This is a real troubling of the Church which shows signs of leading to a perversion of the Gospel of Christ, and it prevents the Church from undertaking real discipline of the minds of its sons and daughters, a discipline which is of greater importance for our whole civilization than the Church has recently dared to claim.'[69]

Nevertheless Hoskyns saw Loisy as in the end sitting lightly to the results of his own criticism 'because the Church was an altogether bigger thing than the particular beliefs and practices of Primitive Christianity.' Certainly, 'Loisy still held the Jesus of history to be important, but in such a manner as to relieve us of the sense of His ultimate authority.'[70] From the later vantage point of this letter, written in 1934, Hoskyns was critical on three further points. The first was of Loisy's own position as a scholar; he thought that in Loisy's commentary on the Fourth Gospel most of the real problems were disregarded. The second was of the inadequacy of Vidler's treatment of the influence of Roman Catholic Modernism upon English biblical studies, and the third was of Vidler's book as a whole as one that 'was not written by a man who has felt where the shoe is actually pinching in New Testament work, or indeed where it has pinched in those long years since the publication of *Das Wesen des Christentums*.'[71] Vidler in reply expressed surprise that in a volume like *Essays Catholic and Critical*, designed to reconcile Catholicism and critical study, a more detailed reference to Loisy had not been made. 'I still think that to treat the aspect of Catholic Modernism with which you were concerned as simply a reflection of the Liberal Protestant reconstruction of Christian origins involves a serious depreciation of the position of Loisy, as also of Tyrrell and Heiler, — and that in the very limited space at your disposal it would have been possible to give a juster account of the difference between the Liberal Protestant and the Catholic Modernist reconstructions.' Further he affirmed that it was not desirable 'that the religious and intellectual challenge of Catholic theology should be bound up with, and made to depend upon, one particular reconstruction of the history of Christian origins,'[72] as Hoskyns had appeared to maintain.

The difficulty of assessing this correspondence is that it was written in 1934 at a time when Hoskyns' attitude to Christian origins would seem to have undergone some further development. He himself half admits that his lack of reference to Loisy had been an omission, but he had also become acutely aware, as he might not have been previously, of the difficulties of Loisy's position and especially of his attitude to the Jesus of history. Vidler, for all his enthusiasm for Catholic Modernism and for Loisy's influence,[73] is also aware of this: 'The gravest weakness of Modernism lay in its willingness to accept without question the radical criticism of the New Testament and the rather wild theories put forward from the side of comparative religion, while "the Jesus of History" cannot be separated from the "Jesus of Mystery and the Christ of Dogma", to the extent suggested at least by the more advanced Modernists, without a complete breach with Christianity of the historical type.'[74] And it may perhaps be concluded from the correspondence that Hoskyns' attitude betrayed the extent to which his own thinking, for all its Catholic Modernist tendencies, was attached to German scholarship and to the debate over the New Testament as it had been taking place in Germany.

Another Catholic Modernist, who probably stood nearer than Loisy to German scholarship, was George Tyrrell.[75] Hoskyns had attached particular importance to his book *Christianity at the Cross Roads*, his critique of it being perhaps his earliest piece of theological writing.[76] The book was important because it was highly dependent upon Schweitzer for its final conclusions, incorporating into an apology for Catholic Modernism eschatological interpretations of the message of Christ. Tyrrell was not primarily a critical Biblical scholar in the same way as Loisy, but Von Hügel, who had himself led Tyrrell to a scientific study of the scriptures, was attracted to him because of his 'penetrating and discerning emphasis on the more mystical aspects of religion'.[77] This difference between Loisy and Tyrrell can be easily noted by comparing *L'Évangile et l'Église* and *Christianity at the Cross Roads*. *L'Évangile et l'Église* was a carefully argued critique of Harnack's position, obviously composed by a biblical scholar of great learning, while *Christianity at the Cross Roads* was a powerfully worded apology for Catholic Modernism very much bound up with the personality of the author. It is true that both books covered the same ground that 'the Christ of eschatology is substantially the same as the Christ of Catholic tradition and experience, that is a supernatural, otherworldly, transcendent, essentially mysterious Christ. But it is exactly these characteristics of the original Gospel and of Catholicism too that are most alien to the modern [Liberal Protestant] outlook.'[78] But Tyrrell seemed to be a writer who was able 'to wield flame rather than words'.[79] His account was full of rhetorical phrases, especially with regard to Liberal Protestantism: 'No sooner was the Light of the World kindled than it was put under a bushel. The Pearl of Great Price fell into the dustheap of Catholicism . . . They wanted to bring Jesus into the nineteenth century as the Incarnation of its ideal of Divine Righteousness. . . . They wanted to acquit Him of that exclusive and earth-scorning otherworldliness. . . . With eyes thus preoccupied they could only find the German in the Jew, a moralist in a visionary, a professor in a prophet, the nineteenth century in the first, the natural in the supernatural. Christ was the ideal man, the Kingdom of Heaven, the ideal humanity.'[80] Tyrrell was also critical of Harnack's picture of Christ: 'The Christ that Harnack sees, looking back through nineteen centuries of Catholic darkness, is only the reflection of a Liberal Protestant face, seen at the bottom of a deep well.'[81] Tyrrell's account then went on to correlate Catholicism and the Gospel much more definitely and confidently than Loisy had done, but it was not particularly good scholarship, and so *L'Évangile et l'Église* remains, in the words of Tyrrell himself, 'the classical exposition of Catholic Modernism'.[82]

Hoskyns' evaluation of *Christianity at the Cross Roads* was that it was 'a book for the moment, not a book that will last; it springs out of the modern historical problems of today, it is a twig on a tree not an independent growth.'[83] This was not meant to make the book any less important, but it had to be understood within the historical context from which it arose, Tyrrell's position as an apologist rather than a critic being carefully noted. Tyrrell saw clearly that in the eschatological school of criticism lay the defence of Catholicism, and he used this to support his own claim that 'if this was the Gospel, if this was the historic Jesus, then in history the Gospel is preserved intact in Catholicism and Catholicism = Christianity.'[84] Hoskyns concluded his article by noting that his purpose had been to explain the circumstances under which Tyrrell wrote his book, which remains meaningless unless the enemies whom he was attacking, and the source whence he got his weapons to attack them, are known.

Hoskyns, in writing to Vidler,[85] spoke of his own particular debt to Weiss[86] and Schweitzer, who had both been used by Loisy and Tyrrell.[87] First published in 1892, Weiss' *Die Predigt Jesu vom Reiche Gottes* marked a significant point in New Testament scholarship because, in the view of his latest English editor, Weiss, together with Schweitzer, 'turned the entire course of Jesus research and undermined the foundations of the

prevailing Protestant theology,'[88] and 'when the eschatological beliefs of
Jesus were taken seriously, it was no longer possible for modern interpreters to fashion the ''historical Jesus'' after their own images, as had
been the custom among the nineteenth-century writers of ''lives of
Jesus''.'[89] Rudolf Bultmann likewise praised Weiss as 'one of the
founders of the eschatological movement in critical theology. . . . Here
a consistent and comprehensive understanding of the eschatological
character of the person and proclamation of Jesus was achieved and the
course of further research definitively indicated. . . . Johannes Weiss'
judgement on the matter has prevailed triumphantly.'[90] The core of
Weiss' argument was that 'the actualization of the Kingdom of God is
not a matter for human initiative, but entirely a matter of God's initiative.'[91] Jesus never thought of the Kingdom of God as 'something
subjective, inward, or spiritual, but it is always the objective messianic
Kingdom, which usually is pictured as a territory into which one enters,
or as a land in which one has a share, or as a treasure which comes down
from heaven.'[92] Although Hoskyns believed that Weiss had been responsible for the initial overthrow of the Liberal Protestant position and for
the establishment of the eschatological interpretation of the Gospel,
nevertheless he complained 'that Weiss had slipped back and joined the
rest of the Liberals; and the field was left open. And Schweitzer had
stepped into his place.'[93]

So it was Schweitzer[94] that Hoskyns held in higher honour. C.K.
Barrett notes that 'one of my greatest teachers, E.C. Hoskyns, was a
friend of Schweitzer's and understood him well.'[95] It was certain that
Hoskyns 'had been influenced by Schweitzer'[96] and that it was
Schweitzer's views which lay behind Hoskyns' essay in *Essays Catholic
and Critical*.[97] Hoskyns' debt to Schweitzer and his eschatological interpretation of the Gospel remained permanent, as comes out for example
in a course of sermons in his College Chapel where he attempted to
expound the significance of eschatology to a lay audience. 'The one
fundamental moral problem is what we should still possess if the whole
of our world were destroyed tomorrow, and we stood naked before
God. The eschatological belief crudely and ruthlessly sweeps away all
our moral busynesses, strips us naked of worldly possessions and worldly
entanglements and asks what survives the catastrophe.'[98] This debt has
gone back to the beginning; from his earliest period Hoskyns had seen
Schweitzer as the most important scholar of his day (c. 1910)[99] and had
noted that many of the articles and reviews against Schweitzer had
missed the real point. 'They never got beyond the apocalyptic side. But

the real value of his book [*Von Reimarus zu Wrede*] is his throwing back the sacramentalism and christology of the early Church on to our Lord himself. He shows that our Lord is really the founder of Christianity — not the apostles, or St Paul, or Alexandrian philosophy or anything else.'[100] It was Schweitzer's ability to look at the subject afresh, undeterred by the claims of ecclesiastical loyalty or the fear of what disastrous consequences his discoveries might provoke, which attracted Hoskyns to him, because 'it is his personal unorthodoxy which makes him so important.'[101]

Schweitzer's general argument was that Jesus as a learned Jew would be deeply versed in Jewish eschatology, and his own religious thought was inevitably based on this: 'There is silence all around. The Baptist appears, and cries: "Repent, for the Kingdom of Heaven is at hand." Soon after that comes Jesus and in the knowledge that He is the coming Son of Man lays hold of the wheel of the world to set it moving on that last revolution, which is to bring all ordinary history to a close. It refuses to turn, and He throws Himself upon it. Then it does turn, and crushes Him.'[102] With this state of eschatological expectation in the mind of Jesus, 'we must always make a fresh effort to realise to ourselves that Jesus and His immediate followers were, at that time, in an enthusiastic state of intense eschatological expectation.'[103]

The result of Schweitzer's work was expressed by Bultmann: 'Today nobody doubts that Jesus' conception of the Kingdom of God is an eschatological one — at least in European theology. . . . Indeed it has become more and more clear that the eschatological expectation and hope is the core of the New Testament preaching throughout.'[104] Hoskyns, in using that work, appreciated its leading role in establishing the eschatological aspect of Jesus' preaching of the Kingdom of God, and it was with the help of Schweitzer in particular that he worked his way to two major principles: that the Kingdom of God preached by Jesus was eschatological in character and based on current Jewish apocalpytic of his time, and that the portrait of Jesus painted by so many liberal scholars was wholly unsatisfactory. Rather Jesus was a real mystery of unplumbed depths and creative energy, certainly not a reflection of modern idealism. In Schweitzer's own words, which were to become famous, Jesus comes to us 'as one unknown and without a name', as by the shore of the lake 'He came to those men who knew him not. He speaks to us the same word. "Follow thou me!" and sets us to the tasks which He has to fulfil for our time. He commands. And to those who obey him, whether they be wise or simple, He will reveal Himself in the toils, the conflicts, the sufferings which they shall pass through in His fellowship, and, as an ineffable mystery, they shall learn in their own experience who He is.'[105] Even when historical science has made its indispensable contribution and done its best to reveal the 'real' Jesus, there remains still another dimension of unfathomable transcendence.

NOTES

33. Adolf von Harnack (1851–1930) was professor at Berlin in 1889–1921 and a disciple of Albrecht Ritschl. He was probably the outstanding Patristic scholar of his generation and the major exponent of the Liberal Protestant position. Harnack's main work was a *History of Dogma*, which was a 'highly detailed account of the evolution of Christian doctrine from its beginnings to the Reformation embodying the thesis that primitive Christian belief was transformed under Hellenistic influences' (B.M.G. Reardon, *Liberal Protestantism*, London, 1968, p. 45). Harnack has been praised as a 'supreme teacher-historian' by W. Pauck, *Harnack and Troeltsch*, New York, 1968, p. 17. It is interesting to note how another young scholar, C.H. Dodd, spent a term in Berlin studying under Harnack at about the same time as Hoskyns, but Dodd was to take a different view as 'it is doubtful if Dodd ever deviated to any substantial degree from the attitude to history embodied in Harnack's work . . . he admired Harnack's methods, he shared his deep religious concern. Statements made by Harnack could have been made later on by Dodd; statements made about Harnack could equally well have been made later on about Dodd' (F.W. Dillistone, *C.H. Dodd: Interpreter of the New Testament*, London, 1977, p. 54).
34. Cobham, 'E.C. Hoskyns: The Sunderland Curate', *C.Q.R.*, CLVIII, 1957, p. 291.
35. Introduction from the translator's preface to the first edition, all subsequent quotations from the English translation by T.B. Saunders, *What is Christianity?*, 3rd and revised edition, London, 1904.
36. B.M.G. Reardon, *Liberalism and Tradition: Aspects of Catholic Thought in Nineteenth Century France*, Cambridge, 1975, p. 271.
37. *Modernist Movement*, p. 105.
38. *What is Christianity?*, p. 52.
39. ibid., pp. 51f.
40. ibid., p. 57.
41. ibid., p. 64.
42. ibid., p. 131.
43. ibid., p. 147.
44. ibid., p. 279.

45. Cobham, op. cit., p. 289.
46. ibid., p. 290.
47. ibid., p. 291.
48. A.F. Loisy (1857–1940) was appointed Professor of Sacred Scripture at the Institut Catholique in 1880, but dismissed in 1883. He was excommunicated in 1908 after papal acts condemning Modernism; from 1909 till 1930 he was Professor of the History of Religions at the Collège de France. Unfortunately, after his break with the Church, his biblical work became at times erratic and recklessly conjectural; nevertheless he remains a brilliant and outstanding biblical scholar. Yet Loisy remains an enigma. It has been suggested that at the time of writing *L'Évangile et l'Église* he was 'outwardly Christian, inwardly an infidel' (J. Lévie, *Sous les vœux de l'incroyant*, Paris, 1946, p. 192). Even fellow-Modernists maintain that he was an extreme egoist and, during the Modernist crisis, was a sceptic and an atheist in disguise (A. Houtin and F. Sartiaux in *Alfred Loisy: sa vie, son œuvre*, ed. E. Poulat, Paris, 1960, especially pp. 138 and 158). A.R. Vidler believes Loisy was sincerely Christian in 1902 and accepts his own account in his *Mémoires (Modernist Movement*, pp. 69–139) and *A Variety of Catholic Modernists*, pp. 20–62. See also B.M.G. Reardon, *Roman Catholic Modernism*, London, 1970, pp. 69–109, and 'Alfred Loisy and the Biblical Question', in *Liberalism and Tradition: Aspects of Catholic Thought in Nineteenth Century France*, pp. 249–81. For Loisy's involvement with von Hügel, see L.F. Barmann, *Baron Friedrich von Hügel and the Modernist Crisis in England*, pp. 79–137.
49. The whole context of this book was made more complex by Loisy's own disputes with the Roman Catholic Church and the development of the Modernist movement within it. The publication of *L'Évangile et l'Église*, more than any other single event, precipitated the Modernist crisis, leading ultimately to Loisy's excommunication and his book being described by the Vatican as the 'synthesis of all heresies' (*Modernist Movement*, p. 100). Its force as a counterblast to Liberal Protestantism ought not to be forgotten because 'it was a brilliant piece of work, original and far seeing, and as a reply to the Liberal Protestant case cogent enough' (B.M.G. Reardon, 'Liberal Protestantism and Roman Catholic Modernism', *The Modern Churchman*, XIII, 1969–70, p. 82).
50. A.F. Loisy, *L'Évangile et l'Église*, Paris, 1902, quotations from the English translation by C. Horne, *The Gospel and the Church*, London, 1908. This particular quotation is from p. 11.
51. ibid., p. 13.
52. ibid., p. 59.
53. ibid., p. 64.
54. ibid., p. 85.
55. ibid., p. 96.

40   *Sir Edwyn Hoskyns as a Biblical Theologian*

56. ibid., p. 102.
57. ibid., p. 165.
58. ibid., p. 170.
59. ibid., pp. 210f.
60. *Modernist Movement*, p. 123.
61. W.G. Kümmel, *The New Testament: The History of the Investigation of its Problems*, Eng. transl. London, 1973, p. 446, note 364.
62. *Modernist Movement*, pp. 123f.
63. This debate between Hoskyns and Vidler is quoted by Vidler at the conclusion of chapter 7, 'Lesser Lights and fellow Travellers', in *A Variety of Catholic Modernists*, Cambridge, 1970, pp. 187–90.
64. J.O. Cobham article on Hoskyns, *D.N.B. 1931–1940*, p. 448.
65. This was probably around 1923, as when Cobham heard Hoskyns' lectures again in 1930 he found them 'radically different from what they had been' (*Cambridge Sermons*, p. xvii).
66. ibid., p. xvi.
67. *Modernist Movement*, p. 124, note 1.
68. *A Variety of Catholic Modernists*, p. 188.
69. E.C. Hoskyns, *We are the Pharisees . . .*, London, 1960, p. 79.
70. *A Variety of Catholic Modernists*, p. 189.
71. ibid., p. 189.
72. ibid., p. 190.
73. Vidler, writing to Loisy in 1931, lamented that 'English criticism of the New Testament remains for the most part incurably conservative, and this again creates a prejudice against yourself.' ibid., p. 3.
74. W.L. Knox and A.R. Vidler, *The Development of Modern Catholicism*, London, 1933, p. 187. Perhaps Hoskyns was troubled by the Modernists' apparent lack of interest in the historical Jesus, as, for example, in his letter to Vidler about Loisy: 'No doubt, as you say in your book, Loisy still held the Jesus of history to be important, but in such a manner as to relieve us of the sense for His ultimate authority' (*A Variety of Catholic Modernists*, p. 189). This point is also raised by the editorial, *C.Q.R.*, CLXVIII, 1962, p. 398. After criticism of Bultmann's approach to the historical Jesus, a similar weakness is noted in the position of the Roman Catholic Modernists, 'with their insistence on the Christ of Faith and indifference to the Jesus of History'. When Hoskyns wrote that 'the Church has always a dagger at its heart, for it cannot long escape from its own theme, the theme which it is bound to proclaim — Christ Crucified' (*Cambridge Sermons*, p. 91), and said that a dagger pointed at the heart of the Catholic religious experience position of Spens, the Master of Corpus (see his *Belief and Practice*, London, 1915), 'the dagger was, presumably, what had always threatened that position, namely, that in submerging Jesus within that to which he had given rise, it lacked adequate criteria by which to assess the experience

for what was true and what false development.' C.F. Evans, 'Cruci-fixion-Resurrection: Some Reflections on Sir Edwyn Hoskyns as Theologian', *Epworth Review*, 10, 1983, p. 73.

75. G. Tyrrell (1861–1909) was a native of Dublin and received an Evan-gelical upbringing, but became influenced by the Anglo-Catholic move-ment, was converted to Roman Catholicism in 1879, and entered the Society of Jesus. From 1899 he moved further away from Roman Catholic orthodoxy, and died in 1909 fortified by the last rites of the Church but having refused a Catholic burial. *Christianity at the Cross Roads* was published posthumously. This represented a working out of Tyrrell's own rejection of the Liberal Protestant thesis and of his accep-tance of the eschatological interpretation of Jesus' message and ministry. He was encouraged in this after reading Schweitzer's *Von Reimarus zu Wrede*, 1906. Writing to von Hügel on 9 April, 1909, he commented that 'having finished Schweitzer and re-read J. Weiss very carefully . . . I realise better the full depth of the Loisy-Harnack controversy.' (A.R. Vidler, foreword to the 1963 edition of *Christianity at the Cross Roads*, p. 9). Hoskyns believed that it was a fault of Tyrrell's book 'that he has never acknowledged Schweitzer by name for he owes everything to him' (Cobham, op. cit., p. 293).

   For the story of Tyrrell's life see: M.D. Petrie, *Autobiography and Life of George Tyrrell*, 2 vols, London, 1912; *D.N.B. 1901–1910*, supplement, Oxford, 1912, pp. 542–5, notice by J. Rigg; *Modernist Movement*, pp. 143–81; and, for Tyrrell's involvement with von Hügel, L.F. Barmann, *Baron Friedrich von Hügel and the Modernist Crisis in England*, pp. 138–241.

76. Cobham, op. cit., pp. 183, 288–93.
77. Barmann, op. cit., p. 138.
78. *Modernist Movement*, p. 176.
79. *Christianity at the Cross Roads*, 1963 edition, p. 7.
80. ibid., p. 47.
81. ibid., p. 49.
82. ibid., p. 76.
83. Cobham, op. cit., p. 283.
84. ibid., p. 293.
85. *A Variety of Catholic Modernists*, p. 188.
86. Johannes Weiss (1863–1914), son of the New Testament scholar Bernhard Weiss (1827–1918), was professor at Marburg and Heidelberg. His *Die Predigt Jesu vom Reiche Gottes*, 1892, although only 67 pages long, was one of the first attempts at a consistent eschatological interpretation of the Gospels. This first edition was revised to 210 pages in 1900 with additional excurses and background information refer-ring to the Old Testament and later Jewish concepts of the Kingdom. The quotations which follow are from the English translation, *Jesus'*

Proclamation of the Kingdom of God, London, 1971, with introduction by
R.H. Hiers and D.L. Holland. See also F.C. Burkitt, 'Johannes Weiss:
In Memoriam', *H.T.R.*, 8, 1915, pp. 291–5.

87. Modernist Movement, p. 106 and p. 164, note 2.
88. *Jesus' Proclamation of the Kingdom of God*, pp. viiif.
89. ibid., p. 28.
90. ibid., p. xi. Bultmann was a pupil of Weiss.
91. ibid., p. 132.
92. ibid., p. 133.
93. Cobham, op. cit., p. 292. Schweitzer also detected this weakness in
     Weiss' *Die Predigt*, complaining that 'the book was too short for
     establishing so radical a thesis' and that he had not followed out to the
     full the implications of his theory. He 'comes to a stop halfway. He
     makes Jesus think and talk eschatologically without proceeding to the
     natural inference that His actions also must have been determined by
     eschatological ideas' (Schweitzer, *My Life and Thought*, Eng. transl.
     London, 1933, p. 48). Yet Schweitzer may have exaggerated this as he
     'recognises only Johannes Weiss' account of *Die Predigt* as a genuine
     contribution to our knowledge of Jesus, because Weiss had shown that
     Jesus' message was wholly eschatological' (Kümmel, op. cit., p. 238).
94. Albert Schweitzer (1875–1965), theologian, musician and physician,
     best known for his hospital at Lambaréné, which he founded after
     leaving behind a brilliant academic career in 1913; see J. Brabazon, *Albert
     Schweitzer: A Comprehensive Biography*, London, 1976, and G. Seaver,
     Albert Schweitzer: The Man and his Mind, London, 1948. On Schweitzer's
     New Testament work see C.K. Barrett, 'Albert Schweitzer and the
     New Testament', *Exp. T.*, LXXXVII, 1975, pp. 4–10. Schweitzer's
     most important work was *Von Reimarus zu Wrede*, 1906. Most of this
     book represents a survey of previous attempts at interpreting the life of
     Jesus, and only in the last 60 pages or so does Schweitzer state his own
     views, namely that for him Jesus' message was '*Konsequente Eschatolgie*',
     and that he shared with his contempories the expectation of a speedy end
     of the world and when this proved a mistake concluded that he himself
     must suffer in order to save his people from the tribulations preceding
     the last days. Ulrich Simon's observation is worthy of note: 'I loved the
     final purple passage about Jesus beckoning us as one unknown from the
     other side. I did not realize that this flourish at the end really contra-
     dicted everything that had gone before' (*Sitting in Judgement: 1913–1963*,
     London, 1978, p. 17). D.E. Nineham ('Schweitzer Revisited', *Explora-
     tions in Theology*, 1, London, 1977, pp. 112–33) believes that 'his mis-
     judgements have cost Schweitzer dear. They have meant that in an
     important area of New Testament study — and one which has proved
     the chief focus of interest in the period since he wrote — his views have
     run directly counter to the almost universal current of opinion. As a

result, the speculative and theoretical, as distinct from strictly historical, side of his work has tended to be eclipsed and ignored' (p. 128).

95. 'Albert Schweitzer and the New Testament', p. 4.

96. *Cambridge Sermons*, p. xvi.

97. ibid., p. ix.

98. ibid., p. 37. The reception of Schweitzer's *Von Reimarus zu Wrede* forms an interesting study, see 'The Influence of Albert Schweitzer', appendix A, *Gore to Temple*. F.C. Burkitt wrote a very cautious preface to the work, having already produced an essay betraying signs of Schweitzer's influence, *viz.* 'The Eschatological Idea in the Gospel', *Cambridge Biblical Essays*, Cambridge, 1909, pp. 193–213. N. Perrin believes that 'of all British scholars F.C. Burkitt was the most influenced by Schweitzer's views' (*The Kingdom of God in the Teaching of Jesus*, London, 1963, p. 39, note 2). W. Sanday at first welcomed Schweitzer's views, *Life of Christ in Recent Research*, Oxford, 1907, especially pp. 88ff, but after hearing von Dobschütz's lectures, published a recantation, saying that he had been over-impressed by Schweitzer's 'audacity and exaggeration' (*Hibbert Journal*, 32, 1910, quoted by Brabazon, op. cit., pp. 143f).

99. Cobham, op. cit., p. 286.

100. ibid., p. 292.

101. ibid., p. 293.

102. Schweitzer, *Von Reimarus zu Wrede*, 1906; Eng. transl. *The Quest of the Historical Jesus*, London, 1910, pp. 368f.

103. ibid., p. 384.

104. R. Bultmann, *Jesus Christ and Mythology*, London, 1958, p. 13; see also Perrin, op. cit., pp. 52–6, for the establishment of '*Konsequent Eschatologie*' in New Testament studies. Perrin mentions F.C. Burkitt, B.S. Easton and scholars who contributed papers to a conference of Anglo-German theologians at Canterbury on 2–9 April 1927. In this context Perrin notes a remark of Hoskyns: 'Our New Testament is almost entirely controlled by the thought of God as active and powerful, and the writers show no tendency to regard his activity as an activity within the sphere of developing history, or as the energy which gives movement and life to the physical structure of the Universe. The action of God is consistently regarded as catastrophic' ('The Other-Worldly Kingdom of God in the New Testament', *Theology*, XIV, 1927, p. 253). Perrin also agrees with Bultmann's judgement that 'the Kingdom of God is an apocalyptic concept in the teaching of Jesus. . . . The many attempts to deny this have failed. . . .' (pp. 158f).

105. *The Quest of the Historical Jesus*, p. 401.

3

THEOLOGICAL WORK UP TO 1931

The course of Hoskyns' theological development, from the beginning of his academic career in October 1919 until the publications of his first major book *The Riddle of the New Testament* in mid-1931, is difficult to determine. This is because he was primarily occupied in teaching and lecturing, and wrote only occasional articles or reviews in various journals. Information is therefore limited to the personal reminiscences of those who knew him and to unpublished lecture notes. J.O. Cobham offers a tentative reconstruction of this development:

Hoskyns was seeking to expound the theology of the New Testament largely in terms of Catholic Modernism . . . and to some extent of the *Religionsgeschichtlicheschule* [History of Religion school of thought].[1] He was also under the influence of those who sought to find authority for Christian belief in 'religious experience'. . . . In his lectures he began with the later books of the New Testament and worked backwards, separating the Gospels as giving the religious experience of the Church (here he used Loisy) from the Gospels as giving the authentic teaching of the Lord. And, though in theory he should have worked back to the problem of the authentic teaching of the Lord, in point of fact he hardly ever arrived there. Thus the impression was conveyed that the final authority was the religious experience of the Church . . . But I know that, when in 1930 I returned to Westcott House, and again went to Hoskyns' lectures, I found them radically different from what they had been. He was not only using the language of paradox he had learnt from Barth, but also using the lexicographical method of the *Wörterbuch*. And I think that something should be said of his recovery of the doctrine that the Greek of the New Testament is, in a very significant sense, 'the language of the Holy Ghost'. . . .[2]

It would appear that the two forces noted in the last chapter — namely Hoskyns' membership of the Church, and his intimate acquaintance with German New Testament theology — continued to be in tension. This tension now appears in a movement from the interpretation of the New Testament in terms of religious experience within the Church (Catholic Modernism), and by the use of data from the comparative study of religion (*Religionsgeschichtlicheschule*), to an appreciation of the New Testament in terms of its Hebraic setting and of biblical language as being in some sense unique.

Thus in the earlier lectures referred to by Cobham, entitled 'Theology and Ethics of the New Testament', the method and content were as follows. Hoskyns began by relating the history of the interpretation of the New Testament up to his own time to the problems of New Testament research. He noted how the complete system of Catholic theology claims to be based upon the books of the New Testament and upon the oral tradition of the Church. At the Reformation this harmony between Church and scripture was broken so that a distinction came to be drawn between Catholic theology and biblical theology. Lutheran writers in fact worked upon the same system as Catholic theologians, collecting and using biblical texts to support Lutheranism. At the end of the eighteenth century there was presented the unedifying spectacle of a number of mutually exclusive sects all claiming to be based on the Bible. As a result of the Enlightenment the historical-critical method of biblical study was born, and this tended to emphasise the dissimilarity between various New Testament writers. These differences could be explained historically. However, English theology has been mainly historical in character, the critical problems raised by continental scholars having been too loosely discussed.

Hoskyns' method is to select good presuppositions and to work on them; the most basic being the fact that there is a unity lying behind the whole of Christianity, and that this can be perceived by Christian experience which results from contact with God. Christian truth comes not primarily from doctrine but from experience; there is little unity of doctrine in the New Testament, but rather a single experience of God reflected in the varying dogmas. The best approach to the study of the New Testament is to experience for ourselves the religious experience which is mediated through the tradition of Christianity. Thus when Hoskyns embarks on the discussion of individual New Testament books he begins with the latest developments in the New Testament, those of 2 Peter, Jude, James, the Johannine writings and Hebrews, and then attempts to see what light these shed upon the Synoptic Gospels, the activity and teaching of Jesus which these represent, and the Pauline letters. From this methodology, beginning with the latest and working to the earliest writings to be composed, it is to be shown that all the New Testament writers are working within the same tradition, and that there are no serious discrepancies between later and earlier writings but only different modes of expression. The Catholic Church is shown to be a correct and legitimate development from Jesus. Church tradition is sound and trustworthy because those who transmitted it were supernaturally guided by the Spirit within the fellowship of Christian believers.

Thus in his early lectures Hoskyns is dependent upon two features of Catholic Modernism: the first that there is no sharp division between Jesus, Paul and the other New Testament writers because the Church has been the guardian of sacred tradition; and the second that Christian knowledge is mediated through Christian experience. He frequently refers to Church tradition and Christian experience; for example, he says that John's picture of knowing God does not refer to intellectual knowledge but to an actual experience which involves the keeping of God's Commandments, because in John 'knowing', 'believing' and 'seeing' God are closely connected. Hoskyns is much more cautious about the influence of religious terminology from the ancient world upon the Christian tradition. He does say that some links are possible, for example in discussing *ekklēsia* he notes the uses of the word outside biblical literature, but he is equally emphatic that the mystery religions did not play any significant part in the formation of Christian theology and practice. Even in these early lectures Hoskyns is moving towards his later position that the solution to the problems of Christian origins lay within the biblical corpus itself.*

Hoskyns' contribution to *Essays Catholic and Critical* (1926), entitled 'The Christ of the Synoptic Gospels', still regarded the solution to the problems of Christian origins as being in terms of some sort of Catholic Modernism (although this is quickly passed over), but there is far less emphasis on Christian experience and much more on biblical revelation. A comparison of this essay with the earlier pamphlet *Christ and Catholicism* indicates the development of Hoskyns as a scholar. Unlike *Christ and Catholicism* it is heavily footnoted and makes detailed references to the views of others, especialy continental scholars. In the judgement of one admirer it 'carried his reputation far beyond the limits of the Cambridge Divinity School',[3] and marked the 'turning of the tide in the study of New Testament theology in England'.[4]

Its general thesis was that the so-called 'Historical Jesus' of Liberal Protestantism was unhistorical, and that the teaching behind the Synoptic Gospels was much more complex and Catholic than was generally supposed by Liberal New Testament scholars. Hoskyns begins by

* The summary of Hoskyns' early lectures is taken from the notes of the Ven. J.O. Cobham made at the time.

posing the question of the relationship between Christ and the Church — which he called 'The Problem'. 'For the Catholic Christian *"Quid vobis videtur de Ecclesia*, what think ye of the Church?"' is not merely as pertinent a question as *"Quid vobis videtur de Christo*, What think ye of the Christ?"': it is the same question differently formulated.'[5]

The problem was historical and theological, and raised the question of the link between the teaching of Jesus of Nazareth and the Christ portrayed by St Paul or St John together with the Christ of Catholic devotion. Attempts have already been made to answer this problem, and it was Hoskyns' intention to guide the reader through the debate. He therefore summarised what he called the 'Liberal Protestant solution'. This solution maintained that the essential teaching of Jesus was not to be found in eschatological utterances, 'but in the Sermon on the Mount, and in the parables of the Sower, the Prodigal Son and the Good Samaritan'.[6] Jesus did not claim to possess a divine nature, nor did he foresee any formal mission or intend to found a Church. Paul christianised popular Greek paganism, and so 'Christianity became a mystery religion which tended increasingly to express its doctrines in terms of Greek philosophy.'[7] It was moral superiority which saved Christianity from the fate of other mystery religions, the original and purest form of Christianity being the religion of civilised and united humanity found in the Gospel of Jesus. Hoskyns was here summarising in a short space the views of a number of scholars — E.F. Scott, J.E. Carpenter, W. Wrede, B.W. Bacon, A. Harnack, T.R. Glover and others. Whether or not this is a fair summary is difficult to determine; certainly not all the scholars mentioned held precisely the same views. It may be said, however, that the summary captured the general ethos of Liberal Protestant ideas.

Hoskyns then continued with the solution to 'the Problem' offered by Catholic Modernism. This may be the weakest section of the essay, since Hoskyns' own general thesis might itself be termed a kind of 'Catholic Modernism' or 'Liberal Catholicism'. It is surprising that he did not outline the Catholic Modernist position in more detail, but by 1926 Catholic Modernism was a thing of the past. Its principal biblical scholar, A.F. Loisy, was by then excommunicated and a self-confessed humanist, and in any case some of Loisy's commentaries, although beautifully written, came to rash and unscholarly conclusions about the historicity of the material.[8] Hoskyns admits that the Catholic Modernist solution was 'undeniably attractive' in its attempt to explain and defend

Catholicism on the basis of this historical reconstruction;[9] but he objected that 'critics do not only question the details of the [Catholic Modernist] reconstruction; they judge the whole to have sprung less from a nice historical sense, than from an impatient anxiety to interpret primitive Christianity in terms of modern thought.'[10]

What was needed, therefore, was 'a synthetic solution', because English theology stood at the crossroads, and the time had come for a contribution to be made from that quarter to the study of Christian origins. What then follows can only be described as outstandingly fresh and challenging, and as showing an originality of outlook regarding the English scene which Hoskyns himself said he had learnt from Harnack and Schweitzer, referring at the same time to the recent German studies in Gospel analysis of K.L. Schmidt, M. Dibelius and R. Bultmann,[11] which were later to become standard in their field. He makes his own contribution to the matters under discussion under three major headings: the literary structure of the Gospels; canons of historical criticism; and fallacies in the Liberal Protestant reconstruction.

Of the literary structure of the Gospels, he noted that there was considerable freedom on the part of the Evangelists in their use of sources, the tradition being preserved and passed on by them not in the interest of historical accuracy but for the guidance and encouragement of Christians. In this a peculiar position is occupied by the Fourth Gospel, where it is almost impossible to disengage the tradition from the inter-pretation. A central place was given in the Gospels to the Kingdom of God, which is both present and future, and this was underlined by a Son of man Christology. The problem, therefore, was this: 'Is this complexity due to the existence within the synoptic tradition of various strata of Christian piety with which the original tradition has been successively overlaid, or is the origin of this obscurity to be sought in the life and teaching of Jesus?'[12] Believing that no solution to the problem is possible without strict adherence to carefully defined canons of historical criticism, Hoskyns mentioned five such canons:

1. Passages found in later sources should not be dismissed as necessarily originating at the date of the document in which they are found.
2. Editorial corrections of an older document need not necessarily be bad corrections.
3. If a word is found in a late document it does not necessarily follow that what is expressed by the word is secondary.
4. The distinctive strata cannot be arranged in definite chronological order.

5. Early words are not always accurately reproduced by later translations or paraphrases — for example, the idea of uniqueness found in
agapētos is not well produced by the English 'beloved'.

Finally, in this section Hoskyns noted fallacies in the Liberal Protestant reconstruction, which was based 'upon a series of brilliant and
attractive intuitive judgements rather than upon a critical and historical
examination of the data supplied by the documents'.[13] An impartial
study of these documents would show not only that the supernatural
element in the Gospels 'may have been primitive and original, but also
that exclusiveness, which is so obviously a characteristic of Catholic
Christianity, may have its origin in the teaching of Jesus rather than in
the theology of St Paul.'[14]

Hoskyns then refers to four major governing ideas of the Gospels: the
Kingdom of God; the humiliation of Christ; the *Via Crucis*; and the
new righteousness and eternal life. The Kingdom was definitely
eschatological in character (Weiss, Schweitzer and Loisy), the idea of
human order as transformed by a gradual evolution of the Kingdom
being completely foreign to the New Testament; rather, with Jesus the
messianic Kingdom had arrived and Judaism was fulfilled by the advent
of the Messiah. The humiliation of Christ was of divine necessity; it
preceded the apostolic mission to the world because this was dependent
on Christ's death and glorification; 'of this humiliation the crucifixion
was both the climax and the completion, for by it the Christ was both
freed and glorified.'[15] The crucifixion was not only Christ's glorification; it inaugurated a new order. The disciples of Jesus were to
continue the *Via Crucis* of Christ; the words of Jesus at the Last Supper
initiated the disciples into this way of Christian humiliation, because
they must share in his broken Body and outpoured Blood. With regard
to the new righteousness and eternal life, 'the Synoptic tradition
presumes eternal life to be dependent on moral conversion effected by
belief in the Christ and by incorporation into the body of the disciples of
Jesus.'[16] Therefore adultery and fornication among Christians were not
just lapses from moral law but apostasy from the Kingdom, the Sermon
on the Mount being not a loosely constructed list of ideal moral virtues
but a description of the new messianic righteousness. During the
humiliation of the disciples on earth they must be strengthened by the
promise of final reunion with Christ in his Kingdom, foreshadowed by
his words spoken at the Last Supper.

Hoskyns concludes by noting major contrasts underlying the synoptic
tradition which have been seldom correctly detected by scholars.

However, these contrasts are capable of synthesis and 'do not break the unity of the whole'.[17] The contrast frequently drawn between the Jesus of history and the Christ of faith is not a real one and should be re-expressed as between the Christ humiliated and the Christ returning in glory. The synthesising link here is provided by the title Son of man which is used to describe both the suffering of Jesus (Mark 8:31, Luke 9:58) and his promised return in glory (Mark 14:62, Luke 17:22–25).

A further contrast is drawn between Judaism and the new supernatural order by which it is at once destroyed and fulfilled. This is not a contrast between reformed and unreformed Judaism, nor between disciples of a Jewish *cultus* and members of an ecclesiastically ordered sacramental one. Rather the synthesising link is the inauguration by Jesus of the Kingdom of God on earth which heralds the end of the old order and the coming of the new. This leaves the way open for Hoskyns to argue that there existed a spontaneous Christian development from the crucifixion through the earliest Pauline letters and the Johannine writings to those of the second-century Apostolic fathers. No 'foreign influence' was exerted upon this development, and so 'there seems no reason to doubt that the characteristic features of Catholic piety have their origin in our Lord's interpretation of His own Person and of the significance of his disciples for the world. The religion of the New Testament provides, therefore, a standard by which the Catholicism of succeeding generations must be tested, and which it must endeavour to maintain.'[18]

Thus, while 'The Christ of the Synoptic Gospels' focussed many of the ideas of Hoskyns' previous shorter writings, these are now argued in greater detail, and with explicit reference to the contemporary scholarship with which he was now engaged as a lecturer and teacher. Once more it emphasised the vital link between Christ and the Church. 'What do you think of Christ?' is same question, differently formulated, as 'What do you think of the Church?' The Liberal Protestant position that the development of early Christianity meant a corruption of the original teaching of Jesus was not borne out by critical investigation. On the contrary, when a synthesis of varying elements within the synoptic tradition was made, 'the last step in the historical reconstruction of the origin of the Christian religion is almost inevitable.'[19] This last statement is not altogether clear, and is only partly explained in the following sentence: 'This was the Gospel proclaimed by Jesus, and these were the claims made by the Jesus of history for himself and for His disciples.' It seems that far more needed to be said at this point about the necessary transition from the proclamation of the Kingdom made by Jesus to the proclamation of the risen and glorified Christ made by the early Church. What made the transition, according to Hoskyns, was something which lay at the basis both of the ministry of Jesus and the ministry of the Church, namely Christ's humiliation and glorification. The divine necessity of the humiliation of Christ was to be succeeded by the humiliation of the disciples in the Church. This was to remain one of the major themes of Hoskyns' theology — the death of Christ followed by glorification.[20]

From these major themes Hoskyns argued for the unity of the New Testament corpus: 'The commentator will find the New Testament is one book, not merely because certain documents have been collected together by ecclesiastical authority or by common Christian usage, but because it presumes an underlying unity of faith and experience.'[21] Here more account could have been taken of diversity within the New Testament. There may well be an 'underlying unity of faith and experience' to be detected and exhibited, but this can only be done convincingly if full account is taken of the different modes of thought and expression in the New Testament writings. Nevertheless 'The Christ of the Synoptic Gospels' in its day was a brilliant and cogent essay, and is still not without value; together with other essays in *Essays Catholic and Critical*, it established a sound scholarly basis of Liberal Catholicism for some years to come.

A further contribution to the Liberal Catholic interpretation of the New Testament was made in *A New Commentary on Holy Scripture* (1928), in which Hoskyns wrote his first piece of commentary exegesis, that on the Johannine Epistles. The purpose of his commentary was to show that some Anglican scholars, 'while holding their faith, are determined in approaching the books to give their critical faculty, instructed by all the means within their power, its full and rightful freedom.'[22] The contributors were 'almost united' in their general point of view, the editors adding footnotes where they thought it necessary in order to emphasise this unity, and the whole book was compiled with 'the ordinary reader or elementary student'[23] in mind. Yet with few exceptions the general tone of the commentary seems now to be routine, traditional and reasonably conservative, Hoskyns' contribution being no exception. Although he did refer in the bibliography to some continental writers on the Johannine literature, he relied heavily on Patristic and English commentaries, especially Westcott (1883), Brooke (1922) and Gore (1920). He concluded that the Johannine literature formed a 'distinct and well-defined group within the New Testament', and that this pointed to 'an almost certain identity of authorship' and 'to a common historical situation which needed delicate handling'.[24] This literature also had a theological purpose in so far as it demonstrated that 'Christian salvation was from the beginning dependent upon the manifestation of the Son of God in flesh, and upon His death,'[25] and that this faith had to be worked out in competition with certain false teachers who were opposed to it. Yet these Epistles were not merely controversial documents, they were 'an admirable illustration of the possibility of conducting a controversy in such a way that there emerges from the controversy a simple and direct statement of Christian truth and experience as realised by one whose interests are primarily pastoral and paternal.'[26]

Like his later work on the Fourth Gospel, this commentary on the Johannine Epistles was almost exclusively theological, and moved forward by theological statements. Thus on 1 John 2: 1–6 he commented that 'the universal salvation can . . . only be appropriated by those who obey the commands and imitate the life of him who made the sacrifice,'[27] while 'only one who is perfect in virtue can remain in active communion and intercourse with God, and assist men to attain the righteousness which is His.' Those who shared this righteousness of God were in 'complete opposition to the world, which strives to entice them with its charm', because 'the opposition between God and the world is therefore absolute.'[28] Thus the blurring of the distinction between God and the world so characteristic of some English Modernist thought was untrue to the biblical writers who maintained this distinction. For the author of 1 John the coming of the antichrists (1 John 2:18ff), who like Judas apostatised from the Church, was a sign that the end of the world was at hand; this excluded the commonly expressed view 'that in the Johannine writings primitive Christian eschatology has been entirely displaced by the mystical union with God and with His Son.'[29] Yet the same author was also anxious to show the importance of Jesus as the Christ, the Son of God, for theology and for the practice of the Christian life, and this was vital for any understanding of Christianity. 'Belief that Jesus is the Christ is not merely the acceptance of a dogma; it is creative action by which men have been transformed so radically that the experience is in fact rebirth from God.'[30] This rebirth was 'achieved by the action of the sinless Victim who offered His Blood for our salvation' and who achieved 'the perfect victory over sin'; through this the believer has the 'possession of eternal life'.[31] The author's purpose in composing the Epistle was therefore 'to ensure that those who believe in the name of the Son of God may recognise clearly that this belief carries with it eternal life.'

The second Epistle is close to the first, identical in phraseology but with a more precise situation underlying it. Although the term 'elect lady' was open to various interpretations, it most likely referred to a particular church.[32] Regarding the third Epistle, Hoskyns opposed Harnack's hypothesis that the opposition of Diotrephes to the Elder and his associates reflected a phase in the early history of the establishment of the local episcopate in which the Elder represented the older patriarchal supervisor of an extended area by means of apostolic emissaries, while Diotrephes stood for the independence of the local church, and was one of those who eventually won the freedom they desired and became themselves local bishops. Hoskyns maintained that this reading of the evidence might satisfy Harnack in his devaluation of apostolic authority and Catholic episcopate, but he rejected it on the ground that administrative questions found no place in the Johannine literature as a whole, preferring the traditional view that Diotrephes was one of the deceivers and antichrists who held the docetic standpoint that Christ could not be associated with the flesh.[33]

The exegesis is therefore entirely theological and 'biblical'; how far it can be called 'critical' is a matter of debate. There are no references to extra-biblical material, and terms like 'word', 'life', 'light' and 'darkness' are discussed entirely from within their biblical setting. Moreover, the critical problems of authorship or of the possible destinations of the Epistles are not really faced. He finds it impossible to decide whether the first Epistle was written before, after, or at the same time as the Gospel, and apart from considering Asia Minor as the possible residence of the author, offers no suggestion as to the destination of the Epistles. He prefers to regard them as essentially 'catholic', as being written not to a distinct group but for all Christians. The situation which underlay them was parallel to that behind the letters of Ignatius, and it was a situation which pervaded the whole Church.

Further illustrations of Hoskyns' critical method and of the theological conclusions he reached by its use may be seen both in individual pieces of his own and in his reviews of the work of others. In 1923 he contributed to *Theology* under the general title 'Adversaria Exegetica' a study of Mark 14:28, 'But after that I am risen I will go before you into Galilee.'[34] He began by noting how commentators had left this difficult saying largely unexplained. It was omitted by Luke who knows nothing of post-resurrection appearances in Galilee but rather had Jerusalem at the centre of his presentation. In Mark the saying is rooted in the Passion narrative and it is repeated by the angel at the empty tomb (Mark 16:7), but if the Gospel ends at Mark 16:8 it is difficult to see what it was intended to convey. As used by Matthew, it appears to find its fulfilment in the appearance of the risen Christ to the eleven on the mountain in Galilee, while John has inserted the discourse which immediately precedes the betrayal as a commentary on this saying, but for Galilee has substituted 'heaven', referring to the return of Jesus from this world to the Father. The clue was to be found however in Matthew's understanding of 'Galilee' in the Christophany at the end of his Gospel; there it is the scene of the command of the Risen Lord to evangelise 'the Gentiles' which marks the authoritative starting-point of the universal mission to the world undertaken by the disciples. That for Matthew 'Galilee' denoted the world of the Gentiles can be seen in his editorial work in 4:12–16, where the movement of Jesus into Galilee is regarded as the fulfilment of Isaiah 9:2, which told of the coming of the messianic Ruler.

With this interpretation of Matthew in mind, Hoskyns returned to the obscure Marcan sayings and was driven 'first to accept the historicity of these sayings [against radical commentators who saw them as additions to the narrative made by the evangelist after the resurrection], and, secondly, to discard the literal interpretation of the Galilee saying as giving no adequate meaning.'[35] 'Galilee' then becomes metaphorical for the establishment after the resurrection of the new covenant which would include the Gentiles and be the fulfilment of the prophetic visions relating to the messianic Kingdom 'not by gathering the nations to Jerusalem, but by the risen Messiah and his apostles going forth to the Gentiles'.[36] These conclusions would be strengthened if it could be shown that the activity of Jesus before the crucifixion was motivated by a conscious desire to fulfil Old Testament prophecy, and that the extension of his mission to the Gentiles found a place in his teaching, 'go before' being linked with a similar expression in Mark 10:32 where it means 'going before' to die. Hoskyns concluded that the Marcan narrative[37] did indicate that Jesus acted and spoke as the Christ of prophecy,[38] and that Mark 14:28 was an example of this, in that the immediately preceding words are a quotation from Zechariah 13:7 concerning the striking of the shepherd and the scattering of the sheep. The combination of the quotation from Zechariah 13:7 and the Galilee saying was therefore of vital importance because it showed that the 'humiliation of the Son of Man among the Jews and his Messianic mission to them must issue in his death, which is the formal rejection of the Messiah and of the Kingdom of God by the people of Israel. This will be followed by his resurrection and the mission of his disciples to the world. Only when this is completed will the end come and the Son of Man return on the clouds as Daniel prophetically saw his coming. On this background the sayings preserved by St Mark become intelligible.'[39]

In this brief article some of the features which were to mark Hoskyns' scholarship are apparent. The first is his predilection for the pregnant and obscure saying or passage, the exploration of which proves fruitful.[40] This leads to the conviction that what is complex and obscure in the Gospel tradition does not arise from the later doctrinal complication of what was originally simpler and more straightforward, but rather it is the other way round: namely that it is the obscure which is original and that the evangelists are often engaged in simplifying it. The fact that the tradition has preserved such obscure sayings therefore points to its trustworthiness. The second feature is his conviction that this complexity arises from the fact that the Gospel tradition is penetrated by a certain distinctive and creative Christology, and that in the end this Christology goes back to Jesus himself and his own interpretation of his mission and not to an imposition upon the tradition from a later standpoint. This involved the importance of the Old Testament as a background, perhaps the exclusive background, of the mission of Jesus, and as the basis of this creative fulfilment. This would seem to indicate that Hoskyns was moving away from the approach and findings of the 'History of Religion' school. Comparison with the other religions of the Graeco-Roman world shows that they did not penetrate to the heart of the Gospel tradition to illuminate it. That tradition is in a measure *sui generis* and can only be penetrated from within the biblical tradition, which is distinctive.

These features can be seen in the discussions of a notable Anglo-German group of which Hoskyns was a member.[41] The group came into being as a result of the World Conference of Churches held at Stockholm in 1925, where the then Dean of Canterbury, G.K.A. Bell, 'expressed the desire and the hope that sometime in the future a group of representatives of different countries and churches might meet together for some common intellectual task under the shadow of his Cathedral.'[42] The group met for the first time in 1927 at Canterbury and the subject under discussion was the Kingdom of God. Hoskyns' contribution was on 'The Other-Worldly Kingdom of God in the New Testament'.[43] In it he insisted upon the essential importance of eschatological language in the earliest existing tradition of Jesus' life and in the Pauline Epistles. The problem, however, was first to discover its significance in primitive Christianity and, secondly, to discuss its relevance or irrelevance for modern Christian faith and practice. Hoskyns was only concerned with the first of these tasks. Paul, he believed, was engaged 'in transferring eschatological imagery in order to describe a present and concrete experience', which was that 'the faithful Christians, filled with the power of the Spirit, are here and now being transformed so as to be like the Son of God, and the ecclesia is the concretion in a living organism of the grace of the Lord Jesus Christ, and the love of God in the fellowship of the Holy Ghost.'[44] It remains characteristic of John, of the Lucan redaction of the traditions behind the third Gospel, and of Luke's own material there and in Acts, that the imminent eschatological hope has fallen into the background. This, however, was not because Luke and John 'are confident that they are able to understand and to interpret'[45] eschatology. Luke sees the coming of the Spirit as true eschatology,[46] while John believes that 'Christianity is eternal life here and now, [and] baptism and conversion involve rebirth from above and entrance into the Kingdom of God.'[47] Thus 'this transformation was the great triumph of primitive Christian thought,' as Christianity was changed from being 'a small company of men and women who expected the end of the world to be imminent into the Catholic Religion of men and women who had found God and entered into the sphere of righteousness and truth.'[48] Yet this does not do full justice to eschatological language, because New Testament writers are controlled 'by the thought of God as powerful and active', and 'show no tendency to regard His activity as an activity within the sphere of developing history, the action of God being consistently regarded as catastrophic.'[49] Important as eschatology was for the conception of God as powerful and other-worldly, it was also important for ethical demands. Eschatology swept away 'all secondary moral business, and stripped the primitive Christians, in idea at least, of all worldly possessions and all worldly entanglements. As a result of the eschatology the ultimate moral duties stood out in all their luminous simplicity — love of God and charity to all who were similarly to be bereft of that in which they had so confidently trusted.'[50] These ethics were not interim[51] but ultimate, being born of eschatological faith. Eschatological imagery was therefore 'fundamental to primitive Christianity because it adequately guarded and preserved the other-worldly character of God, of the church, and of Christian morality.'[52]

The group met for the second time in 1928 at the Wartburg above

Eisenach, and the subject was Christology.[53] Hoskyns' contribution was published in note form as fifteen propositions under the title 'Jesus Christ Son of God Saviour'.[54] He maintained that the distinction between fact and interpretation was a false distinction (1), while 'the prime historical problem of Christian origins is to discover the relation between the teaching of Jesus and Pauline-Johannine theology' (3). A mere discussion of the Christological titles provides an inadequate introduction to the Christology of the Synoptic Gospels (4), because these titles can only be adequately interpreted after a careful study of the miraculous narratives, the parables, and the aphoristic utterances of Jesus (5). These also have a soteriological aspect, because the Kingdom of God and Christology are inseparable (9). The death of Jesus was not primarily the death of a martyr in the cause of reform, but a 'redemptive, voluntary, and liberating act', while the resurrection sayings must not be treated merely as 'semi-credal interpolations' (12). The student of the Synoptic Gospels is exhorted not to impose the language of later doctrinal orthodoxy upon the material, but nevertheless this language is latent in the Synoptic Gospels (14). Finally, if this analysis is correct then the Pauline-Johannine interpretations belong to the same world as the Synoptic Gospels (15). Although in note form, these convictions can be seen to be consistent with those already advanced in *Christ and Catholicism* (1923), notably that Christological significance is to be found in the earliest stages of the Gospel tradition and indeed with Jesus himself, and has not been imposed upon the tradition by later interpretations, while basically the New Testament forms a basic unity of thought within itself.

The most substantial outcome of this group, however, was the volume of essays which it was led to produce in order 'to give literary expression to a common theological task', and which was published simultaneously in English and German, under the title *Mysterium Christi*.[56] It contained essays which were to become famous, notably those of G. Kittel on 'The Jesus of History', of C.H. Dodd on 'Jesus as a Teacher and Prophet' and of A.E.J. Rawlinson on 'Corpus Christi'. Hoskyns' contribution was on a key subject, 'Jesus the Messiah', and was his most substantial theological essay up to that time. He begins with the assumption that the centre of New Testament interpretation should be the classical Old Testament, the Law and the prophets, and that there is 'no event or utterance recorded of Him [Christ] which does not wholly proceed from a conception of Messiahship smelted and sublimed from the ore of the Old Testament Scriptures.'[57] Admittedly

the Gospels are the work of Evangelists who were members of the
Church, but nevertheless 'the creative activity rests with Jesus and not
with the Church or with a series of editors.'[58] He notes the recent
developments in the 'form-critical' analysis of the Gospels, but
complains here that 'if the titles [of Jesus] be detached and considered by
themselves they are found to possess no precise meaning;'[59] instead, 'the
significance of the titles and the necessity of the Crucifixion are set
hidden and embedded in the teaching and actions of Jesus, and emerge
only when these are subjected to a careful and accurate analysis.'[60] His
purpose is not so much to discover the literary techniques of the Evangelists as to recover the original words and actions of Jesus. Here, as
elsewhere, Hoskyns works out his assumptions by referring to difficult
and obscure texts. The word *mogilalos* in the narrative of the healing of
the deaf and dumb (Mark 7:32) 'betrays the relation between the New
Testament works of healing and the Old Testament marks of the
Messianic age,'[61] and the crowd who see the healing must look beyond
this to the Christ in their midst. Jesus' healing on the Sabbath (Mark
2:1–6) likewise forms 'a ritual anticipation of the advent of the Messianic
age', and exhibits 'the presence of the Messiah'[62] because the attitude of
Jesus to the Sabbath 'is best explained as a creative Messianic interpretation of the Jewish observance of the Sabbath under the influence of the
Old Testament prophecies of the Rest which God would provide for His
faithful people, rather than as a mere adaptation of ideas already current
among the Jews.'[63]

The moral teaching of Jesus is similarly conditioned by his claim to be
the Messiah.[64] Jesus' argument concerning divorce (Mark 10:1–12) from
Genesis 2:24 is that the righteousness of God leaves no room for divorce;
the contradiction between this and the Mosaic Law (Deut. 24:1–3) is
'resolved not by a gradual moral progress among men; but by that
purification of the heart which of necessity accompanies a genuine acceptance of the call of the Messiah.'[65] Similarly the parables are 'Messianic
hard sayings' betraying originality rather than editorial manipulation.[66]
In every stratum of the tradition which the Evangelists received there is
clear Messianic significance. The Christological titles too have been
given creative interpretation by Jesus himself on the foundation of the
Old Testament scriptures; detached from his teaching they have no clear
or precise meaning. This is illustrated by reference to the titles Son of
God and Son of man. Jesus' use of these titles 'secures the precise
definition of the Messiah, as He is not only wholly dependent upon
God'[67] but must also obey his will to the uttermost. The isolation of

Jesus, the tension between him and the crowds and between him and his disciples, proceeds from and is conditioned by this unique Messianic Sonship.[68] From the notion of tension Hoskyns describes Christ's ministry in terms of paradox, which mainly appears in his death as 'the necessary working out of the righteousness of God quite literally in flesh and blood'.[69] This is seen not merely as the result of the malicious planning of the Jews, but as of divine necessity, and 'was involved from the beginning of His ministry in His creative definition of the Messiahship as the Son of Man. The initiative rested wholly with Jesus Himself.'[70] Finally Hoskyns notes that the purpose of his essay was to make a critical reconstruction of the background of the ministry of Jesus and to claim priority for Christology in theological study. For 'only when the Christology is taken seriously and when its fundamental importance is fully recognised does Jesus emerge as a concrete figure in history. Only upon the background of the Christology do the great *Logia* which lie scattered about in the various literary strata of the Gospels cease to be disconnected fragments and come together as component parts of one messianic whole directed towards the crucifixion and towards the ratification by God of the obedience of the Messiah in resurrection.'[71]

Hoskyns and his fellow-essayists, each in his own way, aimed not only to recover the centrality of Christology in the New Testament, but to illustrate how a doctrine of the Son, of the Messiahship, of the person of Christ, was integral to Christianity from the first, and could not have been interpolated into Christianity from outside. It began with Jesus and his unique interpretation and fulfilment of the Old Testament scriptures. This means that the Christology of Paul and John is far nearer to the Jesus of history than is normally allowed. In his concluding paragraph, Hoskyns allowed himself some reflections on the wider implications of his subject: 'This rehabilitation of Christology is, however, not merely a piece of New Testament exegesis which challenges the adequacy of the ruling reconstruction of the development of primitive Christianity . . . it has implications for Christian Theology and for philosophy which vitally affect the doctrine of the Incarnation. The New Testament scholar, who is also a Christian, cannot patiently permit the dogmatist or the philosopher to expound the doctrine of the Incarnation on the basis of an analysis of human nature illustrated by the humanity of Jesus. He was unique, and this particularly rivets the Christian doctrine of the Incarnation to the Christology . . . and presents awkward material to the philosopher who is operating with a rigid doctrine of evolution.'[72] Thus attempts to restate Christianity in terms of evolution, so making Jesus the highest point in an evolutionary process, were doomed to failure. Hoskyns was here undoubtedly, in company with leading British and German New Testament scholars, helping to turn the tide away from the Christ of Liberalism, away from the Christ who could always be interpreted by means of the comparative study of religions, to the Christ who was in the strict sense unique, and who, as Messiah of God from the first, interpreted his mission almost wholly in terms of the Old Testament.

Hoskyns' own lectures at the beginning of the 1930s followed similar lines. These lectures opened with two definitions relating to the theology and ethics of the New Testament: 'The study of the theology of the New Testament is concerned with the analysis and description of that energetic and specific faith in God which controlled Christian believers in the first century A.D., in so far as the books of the New Testament bear witness to that faith,' and 'the study of the ethics of the New Testament is concerned with the analysis and description of the actual behaviour of those men and women whose thought and actions were, during the first century A.D., controlled by specifically Christian faith in God, and of the nature of the forces which directed their concrete behaviour, in so far as the books of the New Testament bear witness to such behaviour and to such forces.' These definitions, upon which the critical study of the New Testament ought to be based, cannot be fully operative without a thorough knowledge of the Old Testament. This is because the New Testament does not rest upon the prophets or Jewish eschatology or upon Hellenistic mystery religions, but on the whole of the Old Testament. Nevertheless Hoskyns does begin by describing the rise of the historical method of biblical criticism and the place of Harnack, Schweitzer and the Classicists (the 'History of Religion' school) in the New Testament interpretation of the immediate past. As for the last, he noted that the New Testament was pulled out of its isolation in the theological faculties into the history of comparative religion. This movement was primarily connected with Richard Reitzenstein,[73] and in its turn it ushered in Catholic Modernism headed by Loisy, who maintained that the search for the historical Jesus was in the end impossible, and that it was also trivial because the Catholic Church lived not by its fidelity to the Jesus of history but by its sacraments, worship and adoration of the Son of God. Thus Catholicism was heir, on its own confession, to the whole religious experience of mankind and not only to Jesus. Hoskyns found all these interpretations of the New Testament open to grave criticism: they seized on one particular element and made it primary, thus making development within the New Testament the complication of originally simple material.

Hoskyns then divides his material into three — the Synoptics, Paul and John — dealing with each in turn. The study of the Synoptics is done by reference to the word *evangelion*, miracles, Kingdom of God, parables and Christological titles. The ethics are dealt with under the headings of wealth and poverty, the family, and eternal life. Each section is related closely to the Old Testament and there are very few references to any literature other than biblical, or to the work of scholars. His exposition of Paul begins from five Pauline descriptions of Christians: the body of Christ, the building, the bride of Christ, the cultivation of God, and the Church. It continues by examining Paul's experience of righteousness by reference to principal words such as love, righteousness, knowledge and faith, maintaining that the central question for Paul was: Why should a crucified figure galvanise faith in the power of God? The lectures on John followed similar lines. Hoskyns was dissatisfied with the current interpretation of John in terms of Greek thought or as a Christian mystic. The Johannine literature was also analysed by means of its major vocabulary, with words like world, eternal life, hour, spirit, and Word being interpreted against their Old Testament background. Thus the lectures in the early 1930s were based on the assumption that the New Testament can be interpreted only by biblical tradition, and that this is best done by a discussion of major words and concepts.[*]

Thus one of the major factors in the development of Hoskyns' theology during this period was clearly a growing conviction that there were important and significant biblical words in the New Testament, and that analysis of them was the most direct way of interpreting it. This coincided with, and may well have been the fruit of, his interest in the publication of the *Theologisches Wörterbuch zum Neuen Testament* edited by Gerhard Kittel.[74] He was the first to introduce English readers to this work, in an article published in *Theology*.[75] There he maintained that 'there is no proper exegesis of the New Testament which does not depend upon a wrestling with the meaning of Greek words.'[76] These words are highly significant because they contain a secret, and this secret is 'the nature of the relationship between God and man'.[77] There must therefore be 'no escape from a severe and very troublesome linguistic discipline'.[78] Hoskyns asks: Is the New Testament scholar satisfied with

[*] The definitions with which Hoskyns began his lectures are reproduced from a notebook of Prof. C.F. Evans, who heard the lectures as a theological student at Cambridge in 1930–1. The summary of the lectures which follows comes from the same source.

current lexicons? and Does the parish priest, in preparing his sermons, find in modern commentaries an explanation of the biblical words used? He therefore praises the efforts of Kittel and other theologians in Germany who have shown that they are 'acutely aware of the linguistic problem presented by the New Testament, that they have formulated the problem precisely, and that they are now engaged in a courageous attempt to solve it.'[79] Hoskyns then outlined the development of the Kittel *Wörterbuch* from the earlier work of Hermann Cremer;[80] its purpose was 'to make and define the new significance and impress and energy which Greek words received when they were made use of by men whose whole manner of life and thought and speech had been subjected to a disturbance which radically altered both the starting point and the goal of all their judgements.'[81] From the evidence of the then newly-discovered papyri it was clear that New Testament writers did not invent a new language; they used current Greek words; but what was important to note was the content given to a word by New Testament writers compared with extra-biblical usage. An obvious example was *doxa*. Outside the Bible its meaning was 'a notion or opinion or judgement, a conjecture or fancy', but in the New Testament it meant the glory of God, never being used for an 'opinion'[82] and only very rarely for 'reputation'. Thus in the New Testament *doxa* attained a meaning which has precisely the opposite of that in extra-Biblical usage, since it meant neither a fallible human opinion nor an equally uncertain human reputation. In the Kittel *Wörterbuch* the older statistical method was left behind, and the reader was presented with a series of essays to explain why a word changes its meaning in New Testament usage. It does not set out to handle every word which occurs in the New Testament, but only words with some religious or theological significance. The scope of the *Wörterbuch* was illustrated by a summary of the articles on Abraham and *agapē*, and he stated his hope that the work would be of use to English students; furthermore he found it difficult not 'to be envious of a country possessed of a sufficient number of technically trained New Testament scholars able both to perceive the nature of the real problems of the New Testament lexicography and to combine in order to solve them.'[83]

Kittel was himself to pay tribute to his friend's interest in the publication of the *Wörterbuch*,[84] notably in the preface to it, but also in two lectures he was invited to deliver in Cambridge in 1937, entitled 'Lexicographia Sacra'. (Hoskyns was undoubtedly responsible for this invitation, but he did not live to hear the lectures, having suddenly died a few months earlier). At the beginning of the first lecture Kittel described Hoskyns as 'the representative of all that is best and that is most profound in English theology'; for not only was he sympathetic to the idea of the *Wörterbuch*, but 'provided us in his own way with a pattern for our own work. His analysis of the biblical terms *alētheia*, *ekklēsia* and *evangelion* in the opening chapters of *The Riddle of the New Testament* are models of theological description, and as such they correspond with the ideal that we ourselves have ever had before us in the preparation of the *Wörterbuch*. These analyses of Sir Edwyn Hoskyns start with the known philological facts about the history of a word. But they go behind these known philological facts and throw light upon the theological development of the word. In this way Sir Edwyn in these analyses has shown the meaning that a word acquires as the result of its being a Biblical word, the meaning that is peculiar to it when it appears as a word in the language of the Holy Scriptures.'[85] The bases of the *Wörterbuch* are then outlined. The first is the assumption that the purpose of New Testament language is to express what God has done in Christ, because 'there would never be any *kērussein* if there were not the fact of Christ Incarnate, Crucified and Risen . . . New Testament words are thus essentially like a mirror, they reflect the fact of Christ;' therefore 'in such a sense we may rightly claim that the New Testament presents a new language and a new manner of speech.'[86] The lexicography of New Testament language then 'appears to be the means by which we shall be able to discover the real contents of that language and then be able to describe that which the words convey.'[87] In this task care must be taken not to overlook theological depths where they exist and not to invent them where they do not exist.

The second basis is that the number of exclusively biblical words in the New Testament and the Septuagint is small, there being a close conformity between biblical theological language and everyday speech. What however is important is the new content given to individual words: 'It is not the vocabulary itself that was new, but the old vocabulary was employed to express fresh things.'[88] This is especially true of prepositions. Christianity introduced no new prepositions but gave the existing ones new meaning by its combination with a particular dative, as for example *en Christō* or *en tō kuriō*. This is therefore the new reality of Christ 'which alone gives it its extraordinary significance.'[89]

However, it is the Septuagint which exercised 'the predominant preparatory influence'[90] upon the New Testament language. The New

Testament idea of *evangelion* primarily arises from the Septuagint rendering of the Hebrew *bāśar* by *evangelizomai*, which is used in Deutero-Isaiah to represent the proclamation of the sovereignty of God. Also important are the words which have 'been re-created by the Septuagint and which have thereby become new words.'[91] (Here Kittel cites *doxa* as a translation of the Hebrew *karod*, *diathēkē* from *kāboth*, *eirēnē* from *shālōm*, *eulogeō* and *eulogia* from *berek* and *b'rākāh*.) Thus we learn that the 'Old Testament and the Septuagint exercise a primary influence upon the essence of the New Testament language.'[92] But this is not the ultimate element, because 'New Testament terminology is centred upon the person of Christ in no chance or superficial manner, but in the formation of New Testament language very fine and indeed sensitive distinctions are made.'[93] Therefore there has been created a decisive link between New Testament and Septuagint language which would add to the notion of the unity of the Bible; New Testament words have however been given their basic interpretation by the revelation of Jesus Christ.

In his article on it Hoskyns had related the *Wörterbuch* not only to the work of technical New Testament scholarship but to that of the parish priest, and he himself used it in a notable series of sermons in the College Chapel in 1932/3 on 'The Language of the New Testament'. There he expounded 'world', 'neighbour', 'now-then', 'here-there', 'tribulation-comfort', 'the weak and the strong', 'flesh and blood', and 'spirit'. He will long be remembered for his much-quoted words found in another of his Cambridge Sermons on 'Sin and the Church', within a philological discussion on the word 'Church': 'Can we rescue a word, and discover a universe? Can we study a language, and awake to the truth? Can we bury ourselves in a lexicon, and arise in the presence of God?'[94]

Although the *Wörterbuch* has been praised as 'in many ways the most valuable achievement in biblical studies of this century',[95] and from it Hoskyns discovered 'the lexicographical method',[96] nevertheless both the method of the book and its use were later to be subjected to criticism. Thus, in relation to the method, James Barr has maintained that 'it is the sentence which is the linguistic bearer of the usual theological statement and not the word. . . .',[97] and if the word is treated in that way, then it 'becomes overloaded with interpretative suggestion.'[98] Therefore the relation of individual words directly to theological thought is a mistake, and one of the great weaknesses of the *Wörterbuch* 'is a failure to get to grips with the semantic value of words in their contexts, and a strong tendency to assume that this value will on its own agree with and illuminate the contents of a theological structure which is felt to be characteristic of the New Testament and distinctively contrasting with its environment.'[99] Regarding Hoskyns' own attitude to biblical words, R.V.G. Tasker, in a review of his *The Fourth Gospel*, comments that 'he was quite rightly a great believer in the use of Biblical Dictionaries and Biblical Concordances, but he overdid the use of the latter, and in a wholly laudable desire to uphold the unity of scripture he tends to find parallels between the Old and New Testaments, and between different parts of the New Testament, which are not really there.'[100] Barr also analysed Hoskyns' comments on 'truth' at the beginning of *The Riddle of the New Testament*,[101] judging that 'the authors have allowed philosophical-theological and linguistic judgements to mingle confusedly.'[102]

Some aspects of the development of Hoskyns' theological thought may be glimpsed in his reaction to the thought of others as it appears in his reviews of their books. He was opposed to small books which developed their thesis on shallow or unscholarly grounds, as for example D.S. Guy's *Was Holy Communion instituted by Jesus?*, published by the Student Christian Movement.[103] Guy's theory was that Holy Communion was fellowship, and that Jesus, as a Jewish house-father, familiarised his disciples through constant table fellowship with the spirit of the common meal; on the night before he died, in a peculiarly impressive way and with unique utterance, he blessed bread and wine, imparting to them sacramental value and using them to bear witness to fellowship. After his death his disciples continued these common meals which helped to deepen and hallow his fellowship, having in mind meals Jesus had shared with them. St Paul, seeing that the church needed sacraments, enlarged the common fellowship meal of the Last Supper and gave it sacramental significance. Hoskyns criticised this book on three counts. First, Guy's thesis had not been tested by careful exegesis of relevant New Testament texts; secondly, there was little reference to the ideas of new covenant and of the sacrificial death of Christ, upon which the Eucharist was based; and thirdly, the major problem had been missed — namely that of the significance of the Last Supper and of the authenticity and meaning of the covenant saying. The treatment of the subject was quite inadequate and superficial. Hoskyns held the same view of much of the work of the Student Christian Movement[104] at the time, and was opposed to its activity in his College.

Hoskyns was also critical of *The Beginnings of Christianity*,[105] edited by Foakes Jackson and Kirsopp Lake, but on quite different grounds. This was a work which was the very opposite of unscholarly and superficial; it was exceedingly learned and detailed, but Hoskyns believed that its general approach was at fault because 'at the moment when English theology is preparing to make its long-delayed contribution to the study of Christian origins, these volumes represent an attempt to drag it back by posing the problem in terms of literature, rather than in terms of developing religion. The editors think in terms of literary documents, and seem unable to think in any other terms.'[106] In the search for sources in Acts, the editors had found a simple Christology which had been submerged by Luke's literary and 'Catholicising' skill, but according to Hoskyns this had led to some false exegesis, because in Acts there was 'no simple, unmixed "Son of Man" Christology' from an early source, but 'an elaborate David Christology, carefully worked out'.[107] So the editors had missed the point of Acts; the purpose of its author had been 'to show that the Gospel which was effective in his day was the same Gospel which the first Apostles preached with such marked results, and which the Lord himself had originally proclaimed.' Therefore Hoskyns thought that there should have been a third editor who had gained some experience in the mission field and would therefore have been able to assess Christianity at the time when it was beginning to catch the imagination of the crowds and to effect conversions. If English theology was to make any independent contribution to the understanding of the beginnings of Christianity, 'it will be by a careful analysis of Christian religious experience, and especially missionary experience, rather than by a strict adherence to the traditional methods of literary and historical criticism.'[108] On the other hand Hoskyns approved of the chapter by F.C. Burkitt, 'The Use of Mark in the Gospel According to Luke', because it maintained that 'since we do not possess the sources which Luke used in writing Acts, it is impossible to discover them by any process of literary analysis.'[109] He was also critical of the editors' attempt to search for a specifically Lucan Church, a search he believed to be fruitless.

One of the most important reviews was that of Bultmann's *Jesus* (1926).[110] Hoskyns began by referring to Bultmann's recent work on the literary analysis of the Synoptic Gospels (1921)[111] and to his two articles on the Fourth Gospel (1923 and 1925). This again shows him to be well acquainted with theological development in Germany and with Bultmann's thought in particular, and knowledgeable concerning 'form critical'* developments before most other scholars, especially in England. Hoskyns summarised Bultmann's main ideas about Jesus — that he regarded himself as the herald of the advent of the rule of God, assuming the role of an eschatological prophet, also that he regarded the present as the hour of decision, offering a clear and distinct alternative, between repentance and alienation from God. While appreciative of the book as vigorous and well worth reading because it called attention to elements in the teaching of Jesus which had often been neglected, Hoskyns put question marks against some of Bultmann's methods and conclusions. First the book's title gave a mistaken idea of its contents. If it had appeared under the title 'Some Elements in the teaching of Jesus', then it would have been open to very little criticism.[112] Further, Hoskyns thought that Bultmann's evaluation of the synoptic tradition, and especially of the authenticity of the material, was 'open to the very gravest criticism'.[113] Certainly Bultmann's conclusions in *Die Geschichte der synoptischen Tradition* had deeply coloured this book, so that the historical framework of the Gospel narrative was believed to be the creation of the Hellenistic Christian community, with the result that the aphoristic utterances of Jesus, detached from the framework in which they had been preserved, provided the only trustworthy evidence of his life and work. This emphasis on the creative activity of the Hellenistic Christian community had, according to Hoskyns, forced Bultmann to shelve some major questions, such as the possible redemptive significance given by Jesus to his coming death. Similarly Bultmann refused to deal seriously with the claim of Jesus to be the Messiah, regarding it as an imposition of the later Christian community. Bultmann's interpretation was also very individualistic, and any idea of the emergent messianic community had to be relegated to a period later than Jesus.

In 1931 Hoskyns wrote a combined review of three new commentaries on Luke.[114] The review is not of great importance in itself, but it contains a statement of Hoskyns' idea of what may reasonably be expected of a commentary. 'The author may intend to introduce his readers to an intelligent appreciation of the book, without presuming of them any technical knowledge; he may assume a technical knowledge, and set out to break new critical ground; he may write primarily as a theologian and endeavour to use the critical prolegomena in order to

---

* 'Form criticism' involves the analysis of Gospel material into various types, viz. narrative, miracle, parable or other words of Jesus, and attempts to see how these forms or types developed before the Gospel material came into written form. It is concerned with the historical setting in which this development took place.

delineate the faith of the primitive church and address himself to the problem of its nature and of its origin; or he may be concerned to use the critical method in order to encourage and guide the faith of his readers.' Hoskyns then proceeded to set the three commentaries into different groups. Those of Balmforth and Manson were for beginners, while Creed's was for specialists, being similar to and dependent upon Klostermann's; 'although it avoided some of the major theological and historical problems of the Gospel,' Hoskyns believed it to be of great critical importance.[115]

Finally passages may be cited which reveal how Hoskyns saw the work of biblical scholarship as a whole, and what he believed to be its inner sources and motivation. They are eloquent passages, taken significantly from a sermon of uncertain date on 'Biblical Criticism and Christian Activity' in a course preached in the College Chapel on 'Studying the Bible'.[116] Hoskyns first seeks to disinfect the word 'criticism' from the sinister meaning it had come to have and to restore its original meaning of accurate observation. He then proceeds to one of his familiar themes, namely that so far from being an invasion from secular studies into theology, literary and historical criticism had to a considerable extent emerged from theology:

A very good claim may be made that a passion for history and for historical investigation is peculiarly Christian. . . . A passion for history is that desire to discover the truth of what occurred in a particular epoch, and to perceive the meaning of events, because such discovery is recognised to be important, and even vitally important, for the very salvation of those who lived many years or centuries after those events occurred. Now whether such a belief in history exists to any great extent apart from the influence of the Christian religion, I must leave to others to judge. But it is certain that, for the Christian believer, such a recognition of the importance of particular historical happenings is not imposed upon the Christian religion, but is embedded in its very heart. I would venture to hazard the challenging statement that the modern study of history is a direct product of the belief of the Church, and that the passion for history has spread outwards from the Church into the secular field rather than that it was developed outside the Church and then forced unwillingly upon the Christians.

My brothers in Christ, you are bound to be engrossed with the study of a particular history because you are Christians; not because you are matriculated at a university, or because you are peculiarly intelligent, or because you are trained to appreciate the results of a new kind of research, but because your salvation as Christians depends upon it. As intelligent men you will, however, be able to understand that the particular Christian history will not be simple or easy, or at once obvious, and that in matters of religion the truth is likely to be more complicated even than elsewhere. Therefore you will be particularly on your guard against the Fundamentalist simplification, as you will be against a Modernist simplification. [. . .]

I am concerned not with any detailed critical results, but simply to ask you to recognise that biblical criticism is not only in theory a Christian activity, but in actual fact has been a Christian activity of very great importance for the training of a literary and historical judgement, which must be preserved and developed. The Christian is not a dishonest man lurking uncomfortably behind walls which have been almost battered down by the attacks of intelligent unbelievers, and which are threatening to fall and crush him. On the contrary, we Christians have a Christian wisdom behind us which can keep secular enquiry and research within disciplined bounds, because the specifically Christian wisdom is very old, very mature, and very much trained to beware of easy simplifications and superficial philosophies. Now it is precisely the background from which this possible wisdom may grow which is being threatened by Fundamentalism, both Protestant and Catholic.[117]

NOTES

1. The 'History of Religion' School consisted of an influential group of German biblical scholars who, between 1880 and 1920, advocated extensive use of data from the comparative study of religions in the interpretation of Christianity. At first the School confined itself to tracing historical development inside Judaism and Christianity, but it soon came to search for parallels in Egyptian, Babylonian and various Hellenistic religious systems. The main exponents of this approach were O. Pfleiderer, 'the father of religio-historical theology in Germany', H. Gunkel, H. Gressmann, W. Bousset, R. Reitzenstein, A. Eichhorn, W. Heitmuller and H. Windisch. For further details see W.G. Kümmel, *The New Testament: The History of the Investigation of its Problems*, Eng. transl., London, 1973, pp. 245–80 and Neill, op. cit., pp. 157–67.

2. *Cambridge Sermons*, pp. xviff. Cobham first studied under Hoskyns in 1919–23. After a period in Marburg under R. Otto and F. Heiler he returned to Cambridge in 1930 as Vice-Principal of Westcott House and so was able to hear Hoskyns' lectures again.

3. *Cambridge Sermons*, p. viii.

4. J.O. Cobham also, believes that this essay 'marked a turning point in English theology', *D.N.B. 1931–1940*, p. 449.

5. 'The Christ of the Synoptic Gospels', in *Essays Catholic and Critical*, ed. E.G. Selwyn, London, 1926, p. 153.

6. ibid., p. 154. Here Hoskyns refers to Weiss and Schweitzer, and maintains that because of their work 'most New Testament scholars have been compelled to treat the eschatological element in the teaching of Jesus far more seriously' (note 1). Vidler believes that Hoskyns ought

to have mentioned Loisy in this context. *Modernist Movement*, p. 124, note 1.

7. 'The Christ of the Synoptic Gospels', p. 157.
8. An example of what Hoskyns considered to be one of Loisy's rash and unscholarly conclusions about historicity can be found in *The Riddle of the New Testament*, p. 67. Commenting on Mark 14:51, concerning the young man who ran away naked at the time of Jesus' arrest, Loisy recalled Amos 2:16 (*Les Évangiles Synoptiques*, Ceffonds, vol. 2, 1908, pp. 589–91). Loisy denied that Mark 14:51 was a historical reminiscence, and suggested that the incident had been created by the application of Amos 2:16 interpreted messianically. Hoskyns noted that 'just when the reader seems to be standing firmly on palpably historical ground, his position is thrown into question by an interpretation which he may dismiss as fantastic, but which remains none the less disquieting.'
9. 'The Christ of the Synoptic Gospels', p. 158.
10. ibid., p. 159.
11. ibid., p. 163, note 1.
12. ibid., p. 164.
13. ibid., p. 166.
14. ibid., pp. 168f.
15. ibid., p. 173.
16. ibid., p. 175.
17. ibid., p. 176.
18. ibid., p. 178.
19. ibid.
20. *Cambridge Sermons*, p. 93: 'The theme of the Church — Crucificion — Resurrection — is therefore the song which is sung, whether it be recognised or not, by the whole world of men and things in their tribulation and in their merriment.'
    Crucifixion-Resurrection, pp. 92f.: 'It is a strange, a unique, tying together of these two words (Crucifixion, Resurrection) that is described by this use of "and", resembling the use of the "thens", the "wherefores", and the "therefores", by means of which the apostolic writers link with the death the resurrection and exaltation of Jesus, or the lives to which his followers are called (Phil. 2:9; Col. 3:1–12).'
21. 'The Christ of the Synoptic Gospels', p. 178.
22. C. Gore, H.L. Goudge, A. Guillaume, ed., *A New Commentary on Holy Scripture*, London, 1928, p. v.
23. ibid., p. vi.
24. E.C. Hoskyns, 'The Johannine Epistles', article in *A New Commentary on Holy Scripture*, London, 1928, p. 658, column 1.
25. ibid., p. 659, col. 1.
26. ibid.
27. ibid., p. 661, col. 2.
28. ibid., p. 662, col. 2.

29. ibid., p. 663, col. 2.

30. ibid.

31. ibid.

32. ibid., p. 671, cols. 1 and 2.

33. ibid., p. 672, col. 2.

34. E.C. Hoskyns, '*Adversaria Exegetica*: But after I am risen I will go before you into Galilee (Mark 14:28)', *Theology*, VII, 1923, pp. 147–55.

35. ibid., p. 152. My parenthesis summarises a sentence of Hoskyns in the preceding paragraph.

37. e.g. Mark 11: 1–11 fulfilled Zech. 9:9, Mark 11: 15–19 fulfilled Mal. 1 and Is. 56: 7 and Mark 12: 1–12 fulfilled Ps. 118: 22–3.

38. See especially C.H. Dodd, 'Jesus as Teacher and Prophet', in G.K.A. Bell and A. Deissmann, ed., *Mysterium Christi*, London, 1930, pp. 53–66.

39. ibid., p. 155.

40. See also C.F. Evans, 'I will go before you into Galilee', *J.T.S.*, new series, V, 1954, pp. 3–18. Evans believed that Hoskyns' article 'has not, perhaps, received the attention which it deserved' (p. 4), and that 'certain points in his interpretation call for more detailed consideration than Hoskyns allowed himself' (p. 5). Evans concludes that in the end 'we have to choose between two alternatives in any interpretation of Mk. 14:28 and 16:7; either "he anticipates you into Galilee, and there, in the parousia, you will see him" or "he is leading you to the Gentiles, it is there you will behold him" ' (p. 18).

41. For further details, including the names of the participants, see R.C.D. Jasper, *George Bell: Bishop of Chichester*, Oxford, 1967, pp. 65–8. The reports of the Canterbury Conference were published simultaneously in *Theology* (London) and *Theologische Blätter* (Leipzig), May 1927.

42. *Mysterium Christi*, p. v.

43. *Theology*, XIV, 1927, pp. 249–55.

44. ibid., p. 251.

45. ibid., p. 252.

46. This is illustrated by the addition of *en tais eschatais hēmerais* into Luke's citation of Joel 2:28 in Acts 2:17.

47. ibid., p. 252.

48. ibid.

49. ibid., p. 253. Here Hoskyns disagrees with 'a learned and pious professor of divinity who attempted to re-express the Christian faith in terms of evolution'. This probably refers to Prof. J.F. Bethune-Baker, Lady Margaret Professor of Divinity in 1911–34 and a leading Modernist. Hoskyns sees, however, the task of a Christian theologian as one of preserving 'the Christian conception of God from the corrupting influence of the dogma of evolution'. He makes a similar remark during a course of sermons preached in the College Chapel on the subject of

eschatology during the academic year 1926/7 (*Cambridge Sermons*, p. 35).

50. *Theology*, XIV, 1927, pp. 254f.

51. This is probably directed against Schweitzer's theory of 'Interimethics', although Schweitzer is not mentioned by name.

52. ibid., p. 255.

53. The reports of the Wartburg Conference were published simultaneously in *Theology* and *Theologische Blätter*, September 1928.

54. Theology, XVII, 1928, pp. 215–7.

55. *Mysterium Christi*, p. v.

56. Although F.W. Dillistone, *Charles Raven: Naturalist, Historian, Theologian*, London, 1975, pp. 207f., calls *Mysterium Christi* a 'disjointed and unco-ordinated collection, in the editing of which little attempt was made to weave the parts into a unified pattern', he does admit that it forms 'an impressive consensus of faith in the living Christ whatever may be the difficulties of historical reconstruction, a common confidence that the Church, if faithful to its Lord, will share His victory over the world'. In this Anglo-German theological group Hoskyns is placed alongside the most prominent theologians of his day; he would have been able to renew his acquaintance with Kittel at Tübingen and to make his first close contacts with C.H. Dodd, who was to succeed F.C. Burkitt as Norris-Hulse Professor at Cambridge in 1935.

57. *Mysterium Christi*, pp. 70f.

58. ibid., p. 71.

59. ibid., pp. 71f.

60. ibid., p. 72.

61. ibid., pp. 72f. This is done by linking the word with Isaiah 35: 4–6, Exodus 4: 10–12 and Isaiah 55:10.

62. ibid., p. 76.

63. ibid., p. 77.

64. ibid., p. 78. Here Hoskyns used G. Kittel, *Die Probleme des Palästinischen Spätjudentums und das Urchristentum*, Stuttgart, 1926, for establishing the messianic background to the moral teaching of Jesus.

65. ibid., p. 79.

66. ibid., p. 82.

67. ibid., p. 84.

68. ibid.

69. ibid., p. 86.

70. ibid., p. 87.

71. ibid., pp. 87f.

72. ibid., p. 89.

73. R. Reitzenstein (1861–1931), a prominent member of the 'History of Religions' School, was professor in Göttingen from 1914. His early work was mainly philological, but in his *Poimandres* (1904) he tried to

show that New Testament phraseology was largely derived from Hermetic sources, and that the Christian Churches were modelled on Hermetic communities, while in his later *Die Hellenistischen Mysterienreligionen* (1910) he sought to establish the direct dependence of early Christianity on Hellenistic, Mandaean and Iranian ideas.

74. Gerhard Kittel (1888-1948) was professor at Tübingen from 1929 until removed from his post by the French after the Allied victory over Germany in 1945. Kittel was a close friend of Hoskyns, collaborating with him in various Anglo-German theological groups. Hoskyns also sent various of his pupils to study under him. For further details on the vexed questions relating to Kittel's involvement with the affairs of Nazi Germany, in particular his attitude towards the Jews, see R. Gutteridge, *Open Thy Mouth for the Dumb! The German Evangelical Church and the Jews, 1879-1950*, Oxford, 1976, pp. 111-5 and 143-5, and R. Ericksen, 'Theology in the Third Reich: The Case of Gerhard Kittel', *J.C.H.*, 12, 1977, pp. 595-622. For the argument in favour of Kittel, see J.R. Porter, 'The Case of Gerhard Kittel', *Theology*, L, 1947, pp. 401-6, the purpose of that article being 'to tell a tale and to rehabilitate, at least to some degree, the reputation of a great scholar and Christian' (p. 402), because his 'approach to the Jewish question is one of love and respect, springing from a profound knowledge of Jewish history and life. There is no trace in his writings of that racial hatred against everything Jewish which marked official Nazi policy' (p. 405).

The opposite point of view is taken by D. MacKinnon, 'Tillich, Frege and Kittel: Some Reflections on a Dark Theme', *Explorations in Theology 5*, London, 1979, pp. 129-37. MacKinnon believes that 'Gerhard Kittel, initiator of that famous *Theologisches Wörterbuch zum Neuen Testament*, . . . bent the great resources of his formation in "biblical theology", his special familiarity with the Judaism of Jesus' life-time, his consummate mastery of the technicalities of New Testament scholarship, to the seemingly congenial task of developing the theological apologia for the Nuremberg Racial Laws. This he did in a notorious book, *Die Judenfrage*, an achievement constituting one of the most terrible *trahisons des clercs* I have ever encountered. After the war, when he knew he was dying, Kittel sent for his friend and colleague Gerhard Friedrich to beg him continue the *Wörterbuch* to its conclusion. One might have preferred to hear that he had asked his friend to help undo (as far as he could) the ill he had done' (p. 131). 'Kittel's anti-Semitism was a deadly infection, and every student should be watchful for its distorting influence in his most pervasively seemingly *wissenschaftlich* contributions to the study of the New Testament' (p. 135).

For a not altogether accurate picture of Hoskyns' relationship with Kittel after the publication of *Die Judenfrage* in 1933, see G.S. Wakefield, *Robert Newton Flew, 1886-1962*, London, 1971, p. 84, and 'Hoskyns and

Raven: The Theological Issue', *Theology*, LXXVIII, 1975, p. 574, where the statement that Hoskyns grew away from his friend (Kittel) cannot be substantiated. Wakefield later graciously modifies his position over this: see *Crucifixion-Resurrection*, p. 66.

75. This article, 'A Theological Lexicon to the New Testament', appeared in *Theology*, XXVI, 1933, pp. 82–7.

76. ibid., p. 82.

77. ibid.

78. ibid., p. 83.

79. ibid.

80. Hermann Cremer (1834–1903) was professor at Greifswald from 1870. His lexicon was published in Germany in 1872, appearing in an English translation in 1878, with further supplements in 1886. Kittel's original intention was simply to revise the Cremer lexicon, but this was found to be impossible and he was compelled to embark on a wholly new work. However, the purpose of Kittel's lexicon remained the same as that of its predecessor: see *Lexicographia Sacra*, pp. 4–6.

81. 'A Theological Lexicon to the New Testament', p. 84.

82. ibid., p. 85.

83. ibid., p. 87.

84. G. Kittel, ed., *Theological Dictionary of the New Testament*, Grand Rapids, 1964, vol. 1, p. viii.

85. *Lexicographia Sacra*, p. 1. Two lectures under this title were delivered in the Divinity School, Cambridge, on 20 and 21 October 1937. Kittel caused some offence to his audience by wearing his Nazi membership badge.

86. ibid., p. 7.

87. ibid., p. 8.

88. ibid., p. 10.

89. ibid., p. 11.

90. ibid., p. 20.

91. ibid., p. 22.

92. ibid., p. 25.

93. ibid., p. 26.

94. *Cambridge Sermons*, p. 70.

95. *Church of Scotland: Special Commission on Baptism*, Interim Report, Edinburgh, 1955, p. 3.

96. J.O. Cobham, *D.N.B. 1931–40*, p. 449.

97. J. Barr, *The Semantics of Biblical Language*, Oxford, 1961, p. 263.

98. ibid., p. 234.

99. ibid., p. 231.

100. R.V.G. Tasker, 'Review of The Fourth Gospel', *C.Q.R.*, CXXX, 1940, p. 320.

101. Barr, op. cit., pp. 195–7. *The Riddle of the New Testament*, pp. 26ff.

102. Barr, op. cit., p. 196.

103. Hoskyns' review is to be found in *J.T.S.*, XXVI, 1925, pp. 203f.

104. The Student Christian Movement developed out of several independent movements in Cambridge and elsewhere in the late nineteenth century. Its aim was to organise study groups, conferences and camps to bring Christian students of all denominations together. Hoskyns' concern about the ecclesiastical 'liberality' of the Movement may have been inherited in part from his father who, as Bishop of Southwell, wrote to the Archbishop of Canterbury (26 February 1921) about a request from the Movement for inter-communion at their Swanwick Conference. Bishop Hoskyns asked what would be the result 'if this crowd of young students go back to their various schools and colleges with the message that Church Order and Confirmation goes for nothing' (G.K.A. Bell, *Randall Davidson: Archbishop of Canterbury*, vol. II, Oxford, 1935, p. 1042). The Archbishop, while agreeing with Bishop Hoskyns, suggested a diplomatic approach to the Movement; as a result, the idea was abandoned by them (p. 1043).

105. Review in *Theology*, IV, 1922, pp. 298–304.

106. ibid., p. 299.

107. ibid., p. 301.

108. ibid., p. 302.

109. ibid., p. 303.

110. Review in *J.T.S.*, XXVIII, 1927, pp. 106–9.

111. R. Bultmann, *Die Geschichte der synoptischen Tradition*, Göttingen, 1921, Eng. transl. *The History of the Synoptic Tradition*, Oxford, 1963.

112. English title, *Jesus and the Word*, London, 1934. In the 1958 edition (Fontana Books) the editors L.P. Smith and E.H. Lantero note that 'it was felt by both publishers and translators that the title *Jesus and the Word* would convey a more definite idea of the contents and viewpoint of the book than the original title *Jesus*. This change was made with the approval of the author' (p. 5).

113. *J.T.S.*, XXVIII, 1927, p. 109.

114. H. Balmforth, *The Gospel according to St Luke*, Oxford; W. Manson, *The Gospel of Luke*, London; and J.M. Creed, *The Gospel according to St. Luke*, London — all 1930 — reviewed in *Theology*, XXII, 1931, pp. 349–54.

115. Creed disagreed with B.H. Streeter over the 'proto-Luke' hypothesis for the formation of Luke's Gospel. 'It appears to me therefore that Mark must be regarded as a determining factor in the construction of the book from the outset' (p. viii, note 1).

116. E.C. Hoskyns, *We are the Pharisees . . .*, London, 1960. Unfortunately, unlike *Cambridge Sermons*, no clue is given as to their date of delivery except a comment in the preface (p. x) by F.N. Davey that the sermons 'were preached more than twenty-five years ago'.

117. ibid., pp. 76–8.

4

THE RIDDLE OF THE NEW TESTAMENT

Some of the factors in the development of Hoskyns' theological mind and method, and some of his characteristics as a scholar and teacher, came to a head in the publication of his first book *The Riddle of the New Testament*.[1] It is not usual for a scholar to produce a first book which is at one and the same time both an exposition of his subject at a high level for the intelligent non-expert and furthermore something of a pioneer work in its field; or that he should do this as joint author with one of his pupils, in this case F.N. Davey.[2] But Hoskyns' view of the nature and function of biblical scholarship, which was referred to in the last chapter, and his vocation as a lecturer and teacher made it natural that he should do so. That the book achieved outstanding success in its aim is shown by the fact that it still remained in print and influential more than forty years after publication, and that it was translated into some eighteen languages, being one of the few books on the New Testament by an English author to have been widely known and used in Germany. W.G. Kümmel closed his magisterial survey *The New Testament: the History of the Investigation of its Problems* with a summary and discussion of it. Its appeal lay in the liveliness and even excitement with which it presented the analytical processes of New Testament criticism, so that the intelligent reader was able to see them at work; also in the cumulative claim to bring to light by these processes a remarkable unity of thought penetrating the variety of·the New Testament documents, which was to be traced in the end to the historical Jesus himself.

The authors gave the book its particular title because, as they saw it, there is at the heart of the New Testament a riddle in the form of the question: 'What was the relation between Jesus of Nazareth and the primitive Church?' From this other questions arise: 'Was there or was there not a strict relationship between this rich piety and exuberant faith [of the primitive Church] and the historical figure of Jesus of Nazareth? Did the life and death of Jesus of Nazareth control the life of the primitive Church? Or were his life and death submerged by a piety and faith wholly beyond his horizon?'[3] To underline the question — and to the horror of at least one reviewer[4] — the authors began by quoting from the Nicene Creed as evidence that for the orthodox Christian, whether Catholic or Protestant, the Christian faith had its origin in and rests upon a particular event in history. It is therefore not only open to, but by its very nature demands, the exercise of those methods of historical investigation which had been developed in the past two centuries.

In the opening chapter the reader is introduced to the character of the Greek language of the New Testament as a language that has particular nuances not only because it had already been used in the Septuagint to render a specifically Hebrew and Old Testament manner of thought, but also because it had been used to express that thought as having taken concrete form in Jesus of Nazareth. This theme, which would have already appeared in the early articles in Kittel's *Wörterbuch* and was to become dominant in that work as a whole, is here illustrated by an examination of the background and use in the New Testament of the words 'Truth' and 'Church'.

In the second chapter the reader is introduced to the textual criticism of the New Testament, since 'no serious historical work can be undertaken on the basis of texts which may be suspected of being radically corrupt.'[5] The reader is given, in summary form, information regarding the major textual groups — Byzantine, Alexandrian and Caesarean — together with information on the major versions of the New Testament and the texts quoted by the Fathers. The weaknesses of the *Textus Receptus* are outlined and the conclusion is reached that 'textual criticism has shown that there was no serious corruption of the texts of the New Testament between the fourth century and the invention of printing, and that even the *Textus Receptus* would not lead the theologian or historian far astray. None the less, of the large number of interesting variant readings already current during the second and third centuries, the original reading cannot be determined by textual criticism alone. The very subtle problems which they present can be handled, but only by the New Testament historian who is beginning to reach conclusions in other branches of New Testament critical study.'[6]

This last statement leads the authors further into the heart of their argument, as the third chapter is concerned with 'the historical problem' which faces the New Testament theologian when applying technical critical methods to the material in hand. This is illustrated by showing how the author of 1 Peter used Isaiah 53 in the presentation of his Christology, and in particular how 1 Peter 2:21–25 is related to Isaiah 53:4–11. The purpose of this illustration is to show that the author of 1 Peter (naturally other New Testament writers are included here) narrated not mere facts but his own judgement on the facts. This judgement is influenced by the particular significance that he gives to the death of Jesus, which to him was redemptive and sacrificial. His use of Isaiah 53 shows how his picture of Christ had been taken from the prophet's description of the suffering of the faithful slave of God, yet his interpretation is riveted all the time to a particular concrete event in history, the death of Jesus of Nazareth. The chapter concludes by posing numerous questions relating to the methods used in 1 Peter and by other New Testament writers. Do these writers bring into their interpretation of the death of Jesus elements which are foreign to it and are therefore corrupting it? Did the author of 1 Peter invent the identification of Jesus with the suffering servant of Isaiah 53, or did Jesus' ministry demand this identification, and was it perhaps made by Jesus from the beginning? The question is then generalised in the form: 'Is the Jesus of history wholly submerged in the New Testament, or does that history rigor-ously control all our New Testament documents?'[7] Here Hoskyns is posing the question, raised in his mind by Harnack, whether New Testament writers added to the tradition elements alien to the teaching of Jesus. Here, as already in earlier writings, Hoskyns argues that they did not do so, but rather that the later New Testament writers inter-preted factors in the ministry, teaching and death of Jesus which had been there from the outset. Equally, Hoskyns saw the danger of Loisy's position that the historical Jesus could be submerged within the Church to which he had given rise.

If later New Testament writers found no difficulty in using the Old Testament in their interpretation of Jesus, is this also true of the writings of the Evangelists? In chapter 4, the authors note that it is the duty of the historian to trace this interweaving of Old Testament and the Christian tradition to see if there was a time when this did not exist. If this can be shown to be so, and if Jesus can be detached from the Old Testament background, then he can be interpreted within the context of humanitarian idealism or within the context of the popular idea that mankind is moving steadily from a simple to a more advanced state of understanding. If, however, it can be shown that Jesus had from the beginning been interpreted against an Old Testament background, then claims from modern humanitarian idealism will have no place, as this is 'not only foreign to the Old Testament, but is incompatible with it', since 'the Old Testament writers are completely controlled by belief in the particular historical revelation of the living God.'[8] The use of the Old Testament by the Evangelists is illustrated by particular reference to

Psalm 22, and the conclusion is reached that the Gospels were written in order to declare that 'the life and death of Jesus were the fulfilment of the promises made by the living God through the prophets and psalmists of Israel.'[9] This is, however, not the end of the matter. It is not sufficient to portray the Evangelists as editors, writing with a purpose; 'to discover the origin of this peculiar interweaving of the Old Testament with the life and death of Jesus of Nazareth, it is imperative that some attempt be made to go behind the synoptic gospels as they stand, in order if possible to lay bare the nature of the tradition concerning Jesus before it was handled by the editors and incorporated into their narratives.'[10]

This leads the authors to discuss the synoptic problem (chapter 5) as 'a necessary prolegomenon to the reconstruction of that original and particular history which underlies the New Testament writings.'[11] It is argued that Mark was the first Gospel to be composed, and that Matthew and Luke used it as a literary source in the composition of their Gospels. Therefore it is of utmost importance to see how they handled and ordered the Marcan material, with an eye to whether as editors they introduced into the Marcan tradition elements which were alien to it, or whether, as had been often assumed, they 'heightened the Christology, placed Jesus in a more and more supernatural setting and, in fact, paved the way for that "catholicizing" of the church which wholly or almost wholly obscured the memory of him at the beginning of the second century.'[12] The authors (chapter 6) maintain the opposite to be the case: that the Jesus of Matthew and Luke has become somewhat tamed and softened, and brought a little nearer to the ordinary categories of human existence, for nowhere in their process of editing did Matthew and Luke 'heighten Mark's tremendous conception of Jesus. No deifying of a prophet or of a mere preacher of righteousness can be detected. They do not introduce hellenistic superstitions or submerge in the light of later Christian faith the lineaments of Mark's picture of Jesus. They attempt to simplify Mark. He is more difficult to understand than they are. . . . All three evangelists record the intervention of the living God in the heart of Judaism at a particular period of history in the words and actions and death of Jesus of Nazareth: all three describe this intervention in the context of Old Testament prophecy: and all three regard these happenings as one great act of God which his rule inaugurated on earth, and as a result of which those who believe are enabled to do the will of God, are freed from the powers of evil, are forgiven their sins, and are given a confident hope that they will share in that life which belongs to the era that is to be.'[13] What Matthew and Luke have attempted to do is simplify the Marcan material in order to avoid crude misunderstandings. They omitted what appeared trivial, ordered and arranged the tradition so that it could be read more easily in public or private, and improved Mark's grammar and style. What they did not do was to add alien elements into a 'simple' Marcan gospel, so making their own Gospels a product of a radically different understanding of Jesus from that found in Mark or indeed in Jesus himself. Here the authors are anxious to show that later Christians did not lose touch with the actual happenings in Palestine, and that no great gulf is fixed between Jesus and the Church, which on the whole bore accurate witness to the significance of what occurred in Palestine.

In chapter 7 on Mark, the authors turn to the question of Christology. This is because, in the discussion of the editorial tendencies in Matthew and Luke, the reader has been taken back to Mark to discover if he has a distinctive Christology and if his interpretation is merely one among many primitive Christian interpretations of a simple original history. The authors see this Gospel as on the whole reflecting a Son of God Christology, and although this Evangelist rarely used the expression, it was certainly his intention to prove that Jesus was the Son of God. Yet a true understanding of Jesus' filial relationship with the Father can only be reached through recognition of his humiliation, completed in the crucifixion, and vindicated by his resurrection from the dead. Any discussion of Christ's humiliation must be linked with his use of the title 'Son of man' used by Jesus some fourteen times of himself in Mark and applied first to his humiliation and then to his future coming in glory. This Son of man Christology, the authors conclude, 'is not a creation of Mark and is not the result of his manipulation of the tradition,'[14] and in the light of this it is possible to view the title 'the Son of God' in its correct perspective. This is because Jesus' Sonship consisted not merely in a recognition of God as Father (as stated by Harnack and others), nor in his being an evidently supernatural figure who performed unique acts (since for the Evangelists exorcism is not a unique act), but in that which Jesus is seen to be in and through his humiliation as 'the Son of man': namely, the one who, by his life and proclamation, is the means whereby the rule of God breaks into this world from the other world. The authors therefore conclude that the Evangelists, including Mark, have not manipulated the earlier tradition in the interests of a later Christology, and that this Christology was not imposed by them on the tradition but was already embedded within it before any editorial redaction was made. Their claim is therefore that at the base of the tradition of the words and actions of Jesus in the Synoptic Gospels is what they call 'a Christological penetration', which in the Fourth Gospel is made explicit and unavoidable.

The authors then examine (chapter 8), with regard to this Christological penetration, those areas of the Gospel tradition constituted by miracles, parables and aphorisms. Despite the similarities of the miracles to contemporary thaumaturgy, the ways in which they are narrated indicate that for the Evangelists, and for the tradition behind them, they are to be understood against an Old Testament background as evidence of the advent of the messianic age and of the saving power of God over evil.[15] Similarly the parables are not general moral truths, but are shot through with the same Christological significance as the miracles, with their emphasis on something hidden which is to be revealed openly in the future, and with 'the same concentration upon the single historical figure of Jesus of Nazareth, so that the movement of Old Testament simile and metaphor comes to rest in this particular history.'[16] The aphorisms of Jesus can be, and have been, paralleled in rabbinic literature.[17] This however does not account for the authority with which they are spoken and the urgency with which they are pressed home, nor for what lies behind this authority and urgency, which is the advent of the Kingdom of God with Jesus and the moral demand that follows from this. 'The complete fulfilment of the law of God is effected in and by the acceptance of the call of Jesus. This is the salvation of the living God, and bestows his supreme treasure which is eternal life in his Kingdom.'[18] The authors are then able to conclude that 'the material is everywhere Christological, although it remains, none the less, fragmentary and episodic. The three evangelists have done little more than arrange the tradition.'[19]

The authors then turned their attention to the theologians of the New Testament, Paul, John and the writer of the Epistle to the Hebrews, and to the claim made by some that 'whereas the older evangelists and editors of the tradition may be found to be competent historians, no such competence can be credited to the theologians of the New Testament. For theologians are commonly supposed to be moving in a world of their own notions and ideas uncontrolled by any regard for strict historical truth.'[20] Instead the authors maintain that the New Testament theologians would have vigorously protested against this (John, for example, had certainly set his theology within the framework of a historical narrative), and that the claim of the latter to be bearing witness to a historical event cannot be wholly disregarded. As for Paul, it is clear that be believed the death and resurrection of Jesus, which had taken place in Palestine, to have supreme significance for mankind. Paul has a spiritual rather than a fleshly knowledge of Jesus, but this did not mean that 'the object of his knowledge has changed from the Jesus of history to the Spirit of Christ. To suppose this would be to make nonsense of his epistles. As he says, his gospel was the placarding of Christ crucified before the very eyes of his hearers, and Paul's determination was to know nothing but Jesus Christ and him crucified. His description of Christians as "in Christ" can be explained only on the supposition that conversion, if it is fruitful, must bring with it a comprehension of the earthly life of Jesus in the flesh and an actual sharing in his obedience to the will of God.'[21] Therefore, the material Paul was introducing into the tradition was not alien to the teaching and person of Jesus, but the theology of this material was being related continually to the earthly Jesus. With regard to John, it was his intention to defend Christianity against the Jews who denied that the Christ had come, and also against those Christians who, in the interests of an uncontrolled life in the Spirit, denied that Jesus had come in the flesh. It remains true that the fourth Evangelist had wholly recast the discourses and narratives of Jesus of Nazareth, but when 'all had been said about the method which the author employed in bringing out this significance, is what he says so different from what Mark had said or from what is involved in the whole material which composed the earlier tradition?'[22] It is within this question that the riddle of the New Testament lies. If the writing of the second Evangelist is compared with that of the fourth, will there be any great difference between them? The New Testament writers moved against the background of a very particular history, that of Jesus of Nazareth, creating their material from this history and moulding it with their own particular theological emphasis. They were not active independently of this tradition, nor did they create the history which they were handling; therefore they must be treated with the utmost seriousness in any reconstruction of Christian origins.

The authors conclude with a chapter on Jesus himself. While admitting that a biography of Jesus could not have been written, and that it was a mistake to remove individual incidents from the total context of the tradition about him, nevertheless they contend that all the material in the New Testament converged upon one single point and had its origin in one single, isolated, historical event. Thus the emergence of the primitive church is intelligible only on the basis of the life and death of Jesus of Nazareth, for any 'historical reconstruction which leaves an unbridgeable gulf between the faith of the primitive church and the historical Jesus must be both inadequate and uncritical.'[23] This leads to a statement of the final paradox of the matter, namely that 'the action of the living God, which took place in a single human life, carried with it no spectacular display of supernatural power. For in the end, and here the New Testament writers speak with united voice, the action of God took place in complete humiliation and in what appeared to be remarkable weakness. The salvation of God . . . occurred in human faith and temptation and in a single, isolated figure.'[24] In the establishment of their arguments, the authors write as historians of primitive Christianity, whose task it is to be mere hewers of wood and drawers of water. It is the function of the critical historian to act as the slave of the theologian or of the philosopher, as he is the slave also of the simple believer or the equally simple unbeliever. Yet the historian can 'claim the right to present, to the best of his ability, a distinct and concrete historical figure on the basis of a critical method of historical investigation.'[25]

In this conclusion the authors maintain that the historical problem posed by their riddle has been solved, and they can point forward to some of the implications of their study which are beyond the limits of the purely historical method. 'The book ends, as it must end, in an unresolved tension between confidence and hopelessness. It ends confidently because the historical problem has been solved.[. . .] The authors cannot pretend to regard their conclusion merely as a tentative guess at a solution.[. . .] The New Testament documents do, in fact, yield to the modern critical method; and yet the solution of the historical problem does nothing either to compel or to encourage unbelief. There are here no "assured results" of New Testament criticism.[. . .] The historian can help to clarify the issue, but no more. He is unable to decide between faith and unbelief, or between faith and agnosticism.[. . .] Upon the ultimate question of truth and falsehood he is unable, as a historian, to decide.[. . .] Here, then, the historian is driven to lay down his pen, not because he is defeated, not because his material has proved incapable of historical treatment, but because, at this point, he is faced by the problem of theology, just as, at the same point, the unbeliever is faced by the problem of faith.'[26]

The book has two appendixes, one dealing with problems of authorship and dating of New Testament books, the other giving a selective bibliography which has been updated in subsequent editions. Regarding authorship and dating, the authors maintain that the New Testament writers were almost wholly unconcerned with such matters, since no single document is dated, and the historical books, as opposed to the letters, are anonymous. The purpose of such an appendix is to show how delicate and difficult the questions of authorship and dating can be. The primary question is whether these documents do more than bear witness to the life of the primitive Church, but also bear witness to Jesus of Nazareth. Here the authors conclude that their book has been written to 'show that they do bear unmistakable witness to him, and that they are otherwise in the end unintelligible.'[27]

The book was widely acclaimed on its appearance and subsequently. It was said to be an example of 'profound and incisive scholarship'[28] and to possess 'great and abiding value'.[29] Perhaps too enthusiastically and with a degree of misrepresentation, the editor of the German translation wrote that 'in no other work do we find so compact and impressive an exposition of the present state of New Testament science after a century of critical and historical investigation.'[30] Kümmel, in his survey mentioned above, found it an 'extremely impressive picture'.[31] Readers of Hoskyns' earlier writings would recognise in it the repetition of positions previously established, for example that the starting-point of historical research into Christian origins is the relation of the Church and Christ to each other;[32] that the New Testament writers, so far from importing alien ideas into the tradition, were interpreting factors in the ministry, teaching and death of Jesus which had been there from the outset;[33] that the core of the tradition lay in hard and obscure sayings rather than in simple sayings which the authors of the Gospels had complicated;[34] that two governing ideas of the Gospels were the divine necessity of the death of Christ and its necessary reproduction in the disciples;[35] and that Jesus and his mission are not to be set against a background of evolutionary thought.[36] Here, however, these separate theses form parts of, and contribute to, a larger and forcefully argued whole.

The book has, however, also been subjected to criticism sufficiently heavy to require attention in assessing its place and value in the history of New Testament interpretation. First, it may be asked, to what extent was the book dated by the circumstances and the spirit in which it was written? Neill states that it was 'launched as a challenge to so much that was current and accepted in English theology at the time.'[37] It is true that many important works in theology, as in other subjects, have been written consciously or unconsciously to combat a prevailing climate of thought, and have derived from this a part of their force. However, this can also constitute a defect and can warp the author's judgement and argumentation. The climate of thought in this case was, at the time and later, called 'liberalism', according to which the works and message of Jesus, interpreted by modern categories, were pronounced to be primary, while the importance of the person who uttered them was secondary. In the opinion of one reviewer, the authors were reacting against this 'liberalism' almost to the point of fanaticism. 'In the main they react against the humanitarianism of Liberal Protestantism.[. . .] It is almost as if the writers feared that some degree of affinity between the Gospel and humanitarianism might emerge from a more lucid treatment of the ethical aspect of the former.'[38] The book would perhaps have carried more conviction on this score as a work of scholarship if it had contained a more detailed and sympathetic account of the 'liberalism' that was being challenged. One difficulty of a book written, rightly, without footnotes in its attempt to present an ongoing argument to a non-expert reader is that it is difficult for that reader to know if the author is commenting on a general trend or on particular individual writers. In *The Riddle of the New Testament* the reader is often at a loss to know to whom the authors are referring. Which type of 'liberalism' and which 'liberal' authors do they have in mind? Similarly the words 'humanistic' and 'humanitarian' are used without further definition and almost as terms of contempt, and this is hardly overcome by the authors' tardy statement that 'this does not mean . . . that the Gospel is in any sense anti-humanitarian.[. . .] Antithesis between it and modern idealism arises, not because Jesus and primitive Christianity were less human than humanitarianism, but because they are infinitely more so.'[39] However, this element of challenge to liberalism can be exaggerated. As the thesis of the book turned out to be novel, and was presented with a certain freshness of mind and with latent passion, it was inevitably seen as provocative in relation to the general religious ethos of the time. The authors themselves claimed to have been pressed to their conclusions by a rigorous application of historical critical procedures, and what is especially striking is their confidence that by those procedures the historical problem at the heart of the New Testament had been solved. It is on this that they are to be judged.

Hence the second criticism is made in connection with the authors' critical method. One of the difficulties arising here is that this method is confined to the literary criticism of the Synoptic Gospels, with the result that they appear to have an almost fundamentalist attitude to Mark as the limit to which literary analysis and enquiry can go and as the baseline of their research; the reader, in their own words, is 'thrust back upon the Marcan Gospel'.[40] Hence the Marcan Gospel itself remains almost uncriticised, and the description of Matthew and Luke as largely 'editors rather than authors'[41] is inadequate. Ramsey believed this to be an important lacuna in the authors' thesis: 'In his [Hoskyns'] exclusive concentration upon literary source-criticism he was on common ground with those in this country with whom he was arguing. It was in keeping with our insularity that Form Criticism, in vogue in Germany since 1918, hardly made itself felt in England until the nineteen-thirties. These facts, while they diminish the permanent value of Hoskyns' work, do not lessen its achievement as a scientific victory amid the conditions of [that] time.'[42] It may be objected that this is to criticise in the light of analytical methods which had not yet appeared; but Hoskyns was clearly already aware of technical form-critical studies in Germany, as his review of Bultmann's *Jesus* shows,[43] and yet he does not show evidence of this having influenced his own analysis of the Gospel tradition, as it was later to influence that of R.H. Lightfoot.[44] This is all the more surprising since in his earlier writings, and in *The Riddle* itself, Hoskyns may be said to have had a kind of non-technical form-critical method of his own. This appears in his repeated judgement that 'the whole is in the part', by which judgement he placed individual and isolated *logia* or incidents against the background of an already formulated theological tradition in the Church.

As a scholar Hoskyns may be said to have been particularly conscious of the Church as living with and by an oral tradition, which is precisely the situation that the form-critical technique sought to investigate. However, there is little sign of this in *The Riddle*, with the result that the authors may be said to have arrived too easily at the unity of the tradition, and to have paid insufficient attention to its diversities, which could reflect real diversities within the early Church. Furthermore, to have devoted only a single chapter to Paul, John and the author of Hebrews, in an analysis of the New Testament which turns out to be largely devoted to the Synoptic Gospels, inevitably invited over-simplification of the relation of these three theologians to an original Jesus tradition, and of vast and complicated problems to which that question gives rise. Thus Kümmel sets over against his judgement of the book as 'extremely impressive' the criticism that in its search for a unified theology in the New Testament its exercise of the critical method had not been rigorous enough. 'For many historical theses which Hoskyns represents are very vulnerable, and even if his major thesis is accepted, that is that Jesus' personal claim and reality constitute the historical root of the New Testament proclamation, it cannot be denied that not only the three later theologians of the New Testament but also in equal measure the authors of the synoptic gospels have given the earliest message new interpretations influenced by ideas foreign to it which do not in every respect offer the possibility of a unified presentation of the New Testament message of Christ. . . . Consequently New Testament research since its revitalization in the twenties of this century has had to wrestle again and again with this problem.'[45]

This naturally leads to what is the central issue. What has made the book impressive and influential is the claim that the historical method uncovers a fundamental unity of the New Testament which can contain within itself many diversities. C.F.D. Moule, reviewing *The Riddle of the New Testament* thirty years after its original publication, wrote that 'for the period between the wars it turned out to be a pioneer work,'[46] but Moule does not say what it pioneered. Was it the movement which came to be known as 'biblical theology'? If so, does the book come under the same criticism as biblical theology was to do later of having achieved a unity too easily and without sufficient attention to differences and developments? Further on in the same review Moule compares *The Riddle* to the inspired guess of a discoverer: 'It may have reached its conclusion before displaying adequate proof.' And writing much later, Moule maintains that 'part of the strength of *The Riddle of the New Testament*. . . was that, whatever reservations one might have about much of its arguments, it showed the impossibility of analysing out Gospel traditions that made any sense at all, without the divine factor attaching to them. "To dissect" is in this case at any rate "to murder". The divine is inseparably there all along.'[48] But it may be asked how far it is possible to accept the general conclusion of a book if we have 'reservations about much of the argument' and consider that the book reached that conclusion 'before displaying adequate proof'. The conclusions will stand or fall by reference to the arguments the authors have used, and the question can be raised whether their critical method was inadequate, and no longer coincided with what was generally understood by the term 'critical' in scholarship.

This combination of doubt about the authors' method of argumentation and the suggestion that they might have in some measure pioneered 'biblical theology' comes to a head in considering their use of the Old Testament. The authors make a consistent attempt to show that the

Gospels, alike in sayings and narrative, everywhere contain subtle allusions to the Old Testament, and that if this is not recognized no true understanding is possible. For example, the story of the young man (Mark 14:51) who fled away naked at the arrest of Jesus is not merely historical reminiscence, since Amos had written 'that he that is courageous among the mighty shall flee away naked that day, said the Lord' (Amos 2:16).[50] Similarly Mark's short summary of the Temptation is obviously intended to recall Psalm 91:11–13, and the linking of the Temptation with the descent of the Spirit as a dove upon Jesus is held to echo the words of the Psalm, 'He shall cover thee with his pinions, and under his wings shalt thou take refuge' (Ps. 91:4).[51] Again, the Marcan narrative of the stilling of the storm and the calming of a frenzied man 'reproduces the sequence and movement'[52] of several passages cited from the Psalms; here 'it is difficult to think that this general Old Testament background was absent from the mind of the author of the Gospel, and that he did not expect his readers to be aware that the hope of Israel is here being fulfilled.'[53] Further, the authors contend that it was not merely the Evangelists on their own initiative who related the stories in such a way as to connect them subtly and intimately with the Old Testament, but that Jesus himself similarly determined his actions and sayings throughout. Even Jesus' use of the hand in healing seems intended to fulfil a common Old Testament metaphor, and on the same basis the words 'the finger of God' became very significant.[54] It is clear that there developed within earliest Christianity the interpretative process whereby the Old Testament text and the Christian convictions about Jesus were brought together, and doubtless this process began with Jesus himself, but the authors may have seen subtle Old Testament allusions everywhere in the tradition and thus have gone too far. One reviewer comments that 'the book is frequently marred by constant intrusions of the Old Testament, which are in reality irrelevant to the evidence, which points to our Lord's unique Messiahship approximating at certain points to some of the dim adumbrations of the prophets but utterly transcending them all.'[55] Even E.G. Selwyn, who would have been sympathetic to the authors' approach, believed that they failed to discriminate sufficiently 'between deliberate allusions and those that are due to literary reminiscence'.[56] This use of the Old Testament is governed by the authors' 'biblical theology', whereby any major theme of the Bible received its definition by being brought into relation with the death and resurrection of Christ.

In some measure, such a use of the term 'biblical theology' has to be distinguished from the use which later came to be made of it. Hoskyns was always innately suspicious of systems, and was conscious of the Bible as being like life itself — something with rough edges — whereas later 'biblical theology' came to involve a more hard-and-fast conception of the Bible as an interlocking whole in all its parts, to be interpreted from within itself alone.[57] It may still be asked, however, whether the authors were not in fact the pioneers of this 'biblical theology', as they certainly later came to be regarded. Certainly *The Riddle* contains some of the ingredients of 'biblical theology': the emphasis on the historical events as forming the core of the Bible; the distinctiveness of the theology of the Bible and of the concepts from which it is built up; the presupposition of the unity of the Bible, with the New Testament being interpreted almost exclusively in terms of the Old; and the belief that this went back to Jesus himself. What is open to question, however, is their attempt to establish those ingredients and their claim that the critical method has itself revealed 'most clearly the living unity of documents'.[58] The authors may well be correct in their assumption that Christ himself 'provided the integrating centre for the diverse expressions of Christianity,'[59] and that the unifying element in early Christianity was the unity and continuity between the historical Jesus and the exalted Christ. It does not follow, however, that the claim to detect in the early Church features radically different from the teaching and life of Jesus is based on a misuse and misinterpretation of the critical method. Further, the continuity between the earthly Jesus and the exalted Christ may not simply have been read back into the earlier tradition from a later theological or ecclesiastical standpoint, but may have been deeply rooted in Jesus' own self-understanding of his unique Messianic and divine mission.

But this may not be the end of the matter as the authors seem to conclude that it is. J.D.G. Dunn presses the argument when he states that in early Christianity 'the unifying strand remains distinctive but the more it was elaborated the less distinctive it appears to have been.'[60] Perhaps then the authors' reconstruction of early Christianity was too narrow as a result of their insistence on a version of Christianity which was biblically based so far as Old Testament interpretation is concerned, but which also bore the marks of early Catholicism. To begin a book about the riddle of Christian origins with a quotation from the Nicene creed, and remarks about the Catholic Christian who kneels at the words '*incarnatus est*' to show his orthodox belief in the incarnation, invites the question whether this is not to place upon early Christianity a structure and a doctrinal framework which was just not there in the New Testament period and which had still largely to be developed. Certainly towards the close of the first century, with the development of so-called 'early Catholicism', firmer and clear boundaries began to be drawn around Christianity by defining its contents more rigidly, crystallising its faith into set forms, and an increasing institutionalisation of its structures. But to what extent were these features already present in the New Testament? Can a distinctive straight line be drawn between Jesus, Paul, the Gospels of Mark and John, and early Catholicism? Is such a line only the result of later reflection, or was it obvious from the beginning? In seeing the riddle of the New Testament as consisting in the relation between Christ and the Church, the authors have insufficiently considered that there may have been no simple normative form of Christianity in the first century, and in their search for unity have failed to do justice to the fact that the 'surrounding diversity is broad and its outer margins [are] not always readily discernible.'[61]

Nevertheless the strength of *The Riddle* (which certainly secured Hoskyns' reputation as a New Testament scholar) was its insistence in the midst of a great diversity of views that no interpretation of the person and teaching of Jesus which failed to explain the faith of the primitive Church could be true to history. What is perhaps even more important is that its authors raised the question which Kümmel rightly maintains New Testament research has had to wrestle with over and over again — the question of the relation between Christ and the many different strands which make up the Christianity of the Church, a question which lies at the heart not only of New Testament scholarship but of the life of the Church as a whole.

NOTES

1. There has been some dispute as to the respective parts played by the two authors, Hoskyns and Davey. W.G. Kümmel, *The New Testament: The History of the Investigation of its Problems*, Eng. transl. London, 1973, p. 460, note 498, believes that "although Davey's innate modesty and profound respect for his teacher led him to describe his role as only that of amanuensis — he drew an analogy with Papias' portrayal of Mark as the recorder of Peter's memories — he has subsequently acknowledged that the writing was wholly his. He sought the advice and guidance of Hoskyns, and the two of them discussed the book chapter by chapter, so that although the ideas of both men are interwoven in the book, it is

essentially the work of Davey. Davey finally abandoned this view — see C.F. Evans, 'Crucifixion-Resurrection: Some Reflections on Sir Edwyn Hoskyns as Theologian', *Epworth Review*, 10, 1983, p. 71. The style of *The Riddle* bears the marks of Hoskyns' direct manner of writing, whereas the sections of The *Fourth Gospel* which Davey wrote reveal his somewhat rhetorical style and tendency to obscurity. In fact this dual authorship was of 'a singularly subtle and elusive kind' (Evans, ibid., p. 71).

2. F.N. Davey went up to Corpus Christi College, Cambridge, in 1925 and took a second class in the Modern and Mediaeval Languages Tripos in 1927 and a first class in part I of the Theological Tripos in 1929. In 1928 he became a foundation scholar and a pupil of Hoskyns. After ordination in 1930, he served as a curate of St Chrysostom's, Victoria Park, Manchester, and from 1932 was sub-warden of St Deiniol's Library, Hawarden, returning to Cambridge as vicar of St Benet's in 1935. Corpus elected him to a fellowship and appointed him Theological Lecturer in 1937. In 1942 he was appointed Rector of Goddenham, Suffolk, and in 1944 moved to the S.P.C.K. where the stayed for the rest of his working life. After Hoskyns' death Davey edited his *The Fourth Gospel*, published in 1940. Davey himself died on 6 March 1973. G.G. Hopkins believes that Davey may have suffered by identifying himself too closely with Hoskyns and was a fine enough theologian to stand on his own feet, see 'Francis Noel Davey', *Theology*, LXXVI, 1973, p. 226. C.K. Barrett has a moving tribute to Davey in his *The Gospel of John and Judaism*, London, 1975, p. ix, and a biographical introduction about Davey has been written by G.S. Wakefield, *Crucifixion-Resurrection*, pp. 3–15.

3. The popular paperback edition of *The Riddle of the New Testament*, published in 1958, contains additional notes and a more up-to-date bibliography than the original published by Faber and Faber, London, 1931. Although the page numbers are given from this edition, none of the later additional material has been used. This particular quotation is from p. 12.

4. In *The Times Literary Supplement*, 16 July 1931, where the authors of *The Riddle* are also advised 'to discard their thesis and seek the solution of the problem presented by the God-Man Jesus on the basis of the assured results of New Testament criticism' (p. 556).

5. *The Riddle of the New Testament*, p. 35.

6. ibid., p. 46.

7. ibid., p. 59.

8. ibid., p. 61.

9. ibid., p. 74.

10. ibid., p. 75.

11. ibid., p. 76.

12. ibid., p. 83.

13. ibid., pp. 103f. Here is stood on its head the thesis, so ably expounded by Cambridge theologians of the time (notably F.C. Burkitt), that in Mark's

Gospel alone can there be traced a genuine historical picture of cause and effect, whereas the Gospels of Matthew and Luke were essentially doctrinal works.

14. ibid., pp. 111f.
15. Hoskyns, in his *Mysterium Christi* essay, pp. 72–4, interpreted the miracle of the deaf stammerer as a sign of the Messianic age by way of the rare word in it, *mogilalos*, because of its use in Is. 35:6.
16. *The Riddle of the New Testament*, p. 134.
17. G. Kittel, *Die Probleme des Palästinischen Spätjudentums und das Urchristentum*, Stuttgart, 1926, p. 96.
18. *The Riddle of the New Testament*, p. 143.
19. ibid., p. 145.
20. ibid., p. 146.
21. ibid., pp. 160f.
22. ibid., p. 166.
23. ibid., p. 170.
24. ibid., p. 176.
25. ibid., p. 171.
26. ibid., pp. 179–82.
27. ibid., p. 204.
28. A comment by C.H. Smyth in the introduction to *Cambridge Sermons*, p. x.
29. Neill, op. cit., p. 219.
30. Quoted by Neill, ibid., and in a slightly different form by C.F. Evans, *Explorations in Theology 2*, London, 1977, p. vii.
31. Kümmel, op. cit., p. 403.
32. Hoskyns had begun his essay in *Essays Catholic and Critical*, London, 1926, with the assertion that to ask 'What think ye of the Church?' and 'What think ye of the Christ?' is to ask 'the same question differently formulated' (p. 153).
33. *Christ and Catholicism*, p. 3; *Essays Catholic and Critical*, pp. 168f.
34. 'But after that I am risen I will go before you into Galilee (Mark 14: 28)', *Theology*, VII, 1923, pp. 147–55, and his discussion of *mogilalos* in *Mysterium Christi*, 1930, pp. 72–4.
35. *Essays Catholic and Critical*, p. 176.
36. Note the conclusion of Hoskyns' essay in *Mysterium Christi*, p. 89, and a sermon in the series on 'Eschatology', *Cambridge Sermons*, p. 35.
37. Neill, op. cit., p. 219.
38. F.D.V. Narborough, review of *The Riddle of the New Testament*, *C.Q.R.*, CXIV, 1932, p. 305. Perhaps Hoskyns and Davey took some heed of this criticism, see their chapter 'The Humanism of the Fourth Gospel' in *Crucifixion-Resurrection*, pp. 155–75. 'Unlike some modern men, but like the other New Testament theologians and writers, the fourth evangelist derives that understanding of God's will for man, which we may rightly

call his humanism, from his apprehension of the relation between Jesus "the Son" and his "Father" ' (p. 155). On 'liberalism', see A.R. Vidler, 'Christianity, Liberalism, and Liberality', *Essays in Liberality*, London, 1957, pp. 9–28.

39. *The Riddle of the New Testament*, p. 180.
40. ibid., p. 105.
41. ibid., p. 75.
42. *Gore to Temple*, p. 135.
43. Hoskyns' review of R. Bultmann's *Jesus* in *J.T.S.*, XXVIII, 1927, pp. 106–9. He notes the author's use of 'elaborate analysis of the literary structure of the Synoptic Gospels' (p. 107).
44. R.H. Lightfoot, *History and Interpretation in the Gospels* (hereafter 'HIG'), London, 1935, being the Bampton Lectures for 1934, espec. Ch. 2: 'Formgeschichte', pp. 27–56, and *The Gospel Message of St. Mark* (hereafter 'GMM'), Oxford, 1950, paperback edn 1962, espec. Ch. 8. 'Form Criticism and the Study of the Gospels', pp. 98–105. It is interesting to note that, with the exception of their use of the form critical method, Hoskyns and Lightfoot agree on some important issues. They are both suspicious of the view that Mark is a 'plain historical record' while John is theological (HIG, pp. 57f; GMM. p. 6 and p. 16), because 'none of the Gospel writers was able to reconcile completely his belief in the person and significance of Jesus with a purely historical presentation of his life' (HIG, p. 220, and Hoskyns, *Christ and Catholicism*, pp. 3f). They both reject the view that Mark's Gospel represents the gradual education of the disciples by their Master in the understanding of his person (HIG, p. 20; GMM, p. 34). Lightfoot quotes with approval from Hoskyns' *Mysterium Christi* essay ('In the end the particularity of the Old Testament is only intelligible in the light of its narrowed fulfilment in Jesus the Messiah and of its expanded fulfilment in the Church' [p. 89]) to illustrate the background of the messiahship of Jesus as portrayed by Mark (GMM, p. 42), and agrees with Hoskyns that Mark's gospel is better understood by a careful reading of John (GMM, p. 51, and Hoskyns, *The Fourth Gospel*, p. 132).
45. Kümmel, op. cit., pp. 403f.
46. C.F.D. Moule, 'Revised Reviews: IV — Sir Edwyn Hoskyns and Noel Davey: The Riddle of the New Testament', *Theology*, LXIV, 1961, p. 144. Vidler, *20th Century Defenders*, p. 92, believes that Hoskyns must be accounted one of the founding fathers of 'biblical theology'. This view, however, ought to be questioned (see p. 114).
47. Moule, op. cit., p. 146.
48. C.F.D. Moule, *The Origins of Christology*, Cambridge, 1977, p. 137.
49. James Barr, *Fundamentalism*, London, 1977, p. 218, makes this accusation against Karl Barth.
50. *The Riddle of the New Testament*, pp. 66f.
51. ibid., p. 68.

52. ibid., p. 70.
53. ibid., p. 71.
54. ibid., pp. 122f.
55. Narborough, op. cit., p. 306.
56. E.G. Selwyn, Review of *The Riddle of the New Testament, Theology*, XXIII, 1931, p. 231.
57. For further details see Barr, op. cit., pp. 213–34, where he links the rise of 'biblical theology' with 'neo-orthodoxy' and especially with Karl Barth, citing the comment that "Neo-orthodoxy has lost its leadership and initiative, and the biblical theology movement has fallen into severe difficulties. I myself have been one of the severest critics of the misuses of evidence, principally linguistic evidence within biblical theology" (pp. 220f). Also James Barr, 'Trends and Prospects in Biblical Theology', *J.T.S.*, new series, XXV, 1974, pp. 265–82. He believes 'it is unlikely that any Biblical theology of academic status will not neglect to reckon with the theological diversity of the Bible' (p. 272).
58. *The Riddle of the New Testament*, p. 180. Note should also be taken of a later remark of Hoskyns that 'the issue at stake is whether it is or is not satisfactory to regard "diversity" as the characteristic mark of primitive Christianity' (*The Fourth Gospel*, p. 97).
59. J.D.G. Dunn, *Unity and Diversity in the New Testament: An Inquiry into the Character of Earliest Christianity*, London, 1977, p. 369. From a much later standpoint this well sums up a major part of *The Riddle's* thesis: 'The delicate threads which hold together the New Testament documents have been shown to be converging upon one single point.[. . .] All this varied material concentrates upon and has its origin in one single, isolated historical event.[. . .] For any historical reconstruction which leaves an unbridgeable gulf between the faith of the primitive Church and the historical Jesus must be both inadequate and critical. . . .' (compare with *The Riddle of the New Testament*, p. 170).
60. Dunn, op. cit., p. 373.
61. ibid., p. 374.

5

ST JOHN I – THE QUESTION OF
KARL BARTH'S INFLUENCE

It is evident that Hoskyns had early begun to pay particular attention to St John's Gospel, for in 1920/1 he wrote four articles on it, one in *J.T.S.* ('Genesis I–III and St. John's Gospel', April 1920) and three in *Theology* on John 3:1–21; 2:13–22 and 10:1–18 (August and September 1920 and April 1921 under the general title of 'Adversaria Exegetica'). In these latter, the English and Greek texts were printed followed by a verse by verse commentary on the major Greek words used, and then a general exposition made of the passages. The article in *J.T.S.*, aimed at a more scholarly audience, begins by noting that many commentators have missed the suggestive character of the Gospel because 'many words and phrases bear two or even three meanings, and each different meaning carries with it further allusion and suggestion.'[1] This is seen to be particularly true in the contrast which the Evangelist makes between Adam and Christ and so between Christ and creation. Hoskyns' starting point here is John 19:26f. where the dying Jesus commends his mother and the beloved disciple into each other's care. Mary is called *hē mētēr* and *gunai*, and this is compared with Genesis 2:23 and 3:20 where Eve is called 'woman' and 'the mother of all living'. 'Mary, the Mother, is, however, not re-created merely as an individual; the title "mother" implies children, and it is through her that life is passed on . . . because Mary is the mother of Jesus, she will become the mother of those who believe in Him. This second motherhood of Mary is anticipated, whose hour will come when the sacrifice on the cross has been offered.'[2] This link between *mētēr* and *gunai* is also alluded to in Rev. 12. Here the woman is first the mother of the child, who is caught up to God and to his throne, then she is also 'the mother of the Christians, who are called "the remnant of her seed, who keep the commands of God and have the testimony of Jesus" (a phrase which incidentally is Johannine).'[3] This leads Hoskyns back to the death of Jesus who, by his sacrifice as the true Lamb of God, passes on purification and new life to all who believe. 'This idea of re-creation and new birth therefore underlies St John's account of the death on the cross, and Mary herself, as the mother of the faithful, shares in this rebirth.'[4] Hoskyns then emphasises that the betrayal and the resurrection of Jesus took place in a garden. This is especially significant because in the Old Testament *kēpos* is used as a synonym for paradise (Eccles. 2:15 and Ecclus 24:23f.), so 'by emphasizing that the great deeds by which Christian redemption was effected took place in a garden, St John suggests that the events which caused the original fall are here reversed, and once again the Garden of Eden is open to men.'[5] This dependence on the Genesis theme of creation is found at the beginning of the Gospel. In the prologue the vocabulary, style and theology all point to Genesis as the author's starting point rather than Hellenistic philosophy or Old Testament Wisdom literature. Because 'Christianity is the new creation, such a creative act can only be explained by the claim that Jesus was the incarnate Word of God.'[6] The whole of the Fourth Gospel can likewise be seen in the same way because 'St John is dealing with the experience of Christianity, and he asserts that it is nothing less than a new creation. He explains this by saying that the author of the original creation and the author of Christianity are the same — namely God himself.'[7]

The same kind of argumentation can be seen in the article on John 3. Here 'the mystery of purification'[8] is said to underlie the author's thought in the first four chapters. Purification is to be linked with the death of Jesus, as it is throughout the Gospel, being individualised in the incident of Nicodemus which is intended 'to show what claims Christianity has upon educated Jews, who were attracted by the new religion, but feared excommunication from the synagogue, and to impress upon Christians the real meaning of their baptism.'[9] Christians are twice born, once at their natural birth, and again at their baptism, this being 'a direct result of the life, and especially of the death, of Jesus'.[10] Thus 'Christianity is an experience of real contact with God, which can only be described as a new birth, involving, as it does, purification and a new life, which is eternal because the new birth is from God.'[11] Hoskyns concludes by discussing the question whether the author may have borrowed his ideas and terminology from the mystery religions. This is answered in the negative; John has used the Old Testament and Christian experience as models upon which to frame his theology.

The article on John 2 is concerned with the old and the new worship of God. By his cleansing of the Temple, which is strategically placed by John at the beginning of the Gospel, Jesus demonstrates that the Temple had ceased to be the centre of the worship of God and that in the future the centre of Christian worship would be his own risen body in heaven. John does not describe in any detail the nature of the new worship, but it can be supposed that his readers would be aware of the significance of the statement that 'the Body of the Lord' would take the place of the old Temple, as this had been destroyed, and 'the Body of the Lord' was a current Christian expression. Yet for John 'the Body of the Lord' was not thought of as only in heaven, because in John 6 'the Lord gives His Flesh-Body to be eaten . . . for wherever the Christians celebrate the Eucharist the Lamb is with them.'[12] John, however, does not limit worship to the Eucharist; 'to him the whole life of the Christian community is the true worship of God, and the whole Christian community is the Temple of God, in which Christians live, possessing the knowledge of God and eternal life.'[13] The Evangelist, then, had two aims in narrating this incident — to show the destruction of the old worship by the Messiah, who is Jesus, and to suggest to his readers the nature of the new worship by his use of the phrase 'the Body of Christ'. Hoskyns concludes by comparing this account with that in Mark 11:15–19, the latter being no mere cleansing of the Temple but rather the manifestation of the Messiah. Thus the two accounts make the same point, John having taken Mark's account and placed it in a new context to bring out clearly one important aspect of it.

In the article on John 10 Hoskyns is anxious to place this chapter within the context of the thought of chapters 9–11 which he sees as closely related, being linked by the theme 'that the Christians are a community completely distinct from Judaism and from heathenism, and that to be a Christian implies a coming out of the old into the new at the call of Jesus . . . Obliterate the otherworldliness of Christianity, and it ceases to be a religion.'[14] Jesus, 'the true Shepherd sent by His Father, has entered into the fold, where the sheep were enclosed, cramped and confined, and has called to the sheep and led those who heard His call out to the pasturage of God . . . Thus the Good Shepherd leads them out of the world to God.'[15] Hoskyns concludes by noting the triple background of the parable: the life of Jesus, the history of the mission to the Jews, and the conversion of the Gentiles. Here John has brought together fragments of the Synoptic tradition and has reformed them, making them into a complete and consistent whole.

These articles can be seen as evidence of Hoskyns' early interest in John's Gospel, and as a prelude to the detailed commentary he was to write on it. They also reflect in their approach and method the 'religion of experience', which was a hallmark of the Catholic Modernism to which Hoskyns was attached at that period of his life and which was to be found in Loisy's commentary on John. This was to give way in the commentary to a more 'theological' approach, and while Hoskyns was to incorporate into the commentary some of the observations he had made in his articles, reference to the Old Testament was a key factor in his interpretation. He did not develop these early essays in typology further, as some others were to do.

He started work on the commentary in 1923. Although originally intended as one of the 'Westminster commentary' series, it soon outgrew the scope of that series and was eventually published by Faber and Faber in 1940, three years after his death, having been edited by F.N. Davey. Hoskyns had produced a reasonably complete introduction and a revised form of the commentary up to 6:31, the remainder being in an unrevised form written at an earlier period. In some ways these 'unfinished' sections are more valuable than those which were revised; they are less complex and more readable, while the 'completed' sections tend to be detailed, complicated and obscure. Why should this be so?

In his preface Davey describes Hoskyns' method as '*solvitur scribendo*': 'First, he would attack a section, armed only with lexicons, grammars and concordance, and with his mind as far as possible evacuated of all that others had said about the section, and would write down what his study of the text suggested. Then the Fathers (not merely by means of the *Catenae*) — Philo, Josephus, the modern commentators, particularly Westcott, Holtzmann, Loisy, Bauer, Calmes, Lagrange and Bernard, and Strack-Billerbeck — were called in. The commentary now emerging was fashioned and re-fashioned; then written out in a ''fair-copy''. Even so, Hoskyns did not regard this as a final copy, but set it on one side till he should have written the main parts of the Introduction and come to see the wood as well as the trees. By 1930 he had covered the whole gospel in this way.'[16] Evidently a change took place which led to the writing of the introduction and a revision of the first part of the commentary in the form in which it now stands. This is in marked contrast with the second and unrevised part. What brought about this change? Davey attributes it to Hoskyns' work meanwhile in translating Karl Barth's *Römerbrief*, and some account must now be given of this episode in Hoskyns' scholarly career, occurring between his earlier and his later work on John.

It was probably around 1925 that Hoskyns first read Barth's *Römerbrief*, and this appears to have been something of a turning-point for him. According to Vidler, 'thereafter he spoke less and less about religious experience and more and more about revelation. Also we find him increasingly using the paradoxical modes of speech which he seems to have picked up from Barth.'[17] Hoskyns began his translation of the *Römerbrief* towards the end of 1931, completing it in 1933. This has been described as 'a very notable linguistic feat'[18] in which the translator has manifested 'the highest degree that sympathetic understanding of the mind of his author which makes possible translation as interpretation, and not simply as the mechanical transference of thought from one set of words to another.'[19] Yet, as Barth himself reminds English readers in his preface to the English edition, there had been a fourteen-year gap between the original composition of the commentary and its translation into English. That commentary must be set against the background of the theological and political situation at the end of the First World War. In this setting the commentary emerged as a reaction to the 'liberalism' of nineteenth-century Protestantism which, according to Barth, had failed to face the religious and social questions of the time. It fell 'like a bomb on the playground of theologians'[20] because it attempted to question what Barth considered to be the fundamentally erroneous outlook of current religious philosophy, with its positive attitude to science, culture and art, its sympathy with mysticism and its stress on feeling, and rather to affirm the supremacy and transcendence of God, whose infinite superiority to all human aspirations meant the worthlessness of human reason. God's sole revelation is in Jesus Christ who alone mediates divine grace, upon which mankind is utterly dependent, since all human achievement is rooted in sin. Barth declares, as a comment on Romans 9: 1–5: 'God, the pure and absolute boundary and beginning of all that we are and have and do; God, who is distinguished qualitatively from men and from everything human, and must never be identified with anything which we name, or experience, or conceive, or worship, as God; . . . God, the Lord, the Creator, the Redeemer — this is the Living God. In the Gospel, in the Message of Salvation of Jesus Christ, this Hidden, Living God has revealed Himself, as He is.'[21]

To what extent, then, did Hoskyns become influenced by Barth through his work of translation? It would appear that he became the recipient of certain dominant features — among them transcendence, the unworthiness of humanity, crucifixion, paradox and ambiguity — and these can be detected especially in a course of sermons that he preached in 1932–3 on 'The Vocabulary of the New Testament — the Language of the Church'. Hoskyns declares that God is 'the Alpha and the Omega, the Beginning and the End. You will perhaps notice how strictly our Biblical writers hold to that truth. They have no adequate language to describe either the beginning or the end of anything . . . We Christians are, therefore, warned that the goal of human life and of human society is not a known fact on the plane of history from which we can start out thinking and divide men into sheep and goats according as they fit in or do not fit in to our pattern. God is the Judge, He is the End.'[22] Concerning human unworthiness, Hoskyns maintains that 'the Church and theology know that they can only sing the song of the glory of God over their own graves and at the place where they have died. This is the secret of the Church; and can you wonder that those who know this secret tremble when they see scientists, economists, psychologists, Hitlerites, leaders of the Group Movement, Communists, and all those many other confident advisers of men marching with flags flying into the abyss where the Church has already stumbled and fallen? — can you wonder that the Church lifts up its voice and utters its tired, weary warning against human *hubris*, arrogance?'[23] On the crucifixion, Hoskyns says: 'The Church has always a dagger at its heart, for it cannot long escape from its own theme, the theme which it is bound to proclaim — Christ crucified.'[24] The style of the sermons is likewise marked by paradox, ambiguity and contradiction. Hoskyns, in recalling his hearers 'to the Biblical language, to the words in which the Church dares to utter the Gospel of God', notes a contradiction; but it is 'a contradiction of which the Church is fully aware. We have to declare the glory of the ineffable, invisible God in words which have been formed to express visible or, at least, analysable things, and further it is we who have to speak these words, we who belong to the world as it is, to the present time, we who are flesh and blood, we who are men and not God.'[25]

Yet these emphases do not add up to a description of Hoskyns as 'Barthian', at least not in the sense in which that term came to be understood. They are also found in Hoskyns' earlier sermons where he complains of attempts to express the Christian faith in terms of evolution,[26] and where he makes use of paradox.[27] Also Hoskyns' own opinion of Barth is far from clear. He reviewed two books about Barth, by T.L. Haitjema in 1928 and by R.B. Hoyle in 1932, dismissing the latter as deficient for failing to recognise that Barth's work is 'the product of a severe wrestling with the Scriptures'.[28] The former review is more significant because not only does it contain Hoskyns' own summary of Barth's dialectical method, but it compares his writings with those of the French Catholic scholar Jacques Maritain.[29] 'In comparing the two there emerges an uncomfortable suspicion that whereas Maritain might perhaps understand Barth, Barth has as yet shewn no glimmering of a perception of the significance of that Catholicism by which men like Maritain are moved and redeemed.'[30] This could provide a clue to Hoskyns' opinion of Barth. His own theology of God, Christ and revelation were sharpened by Barth's particular tone of speech and mode of expression, but this for Hoskyns had to be understood within the setting of Catholic Christianity, as he understood it, and within the context of his own biblical scholarship. This is emphasised by the letter Hoskyns wrote to Barth on his fiftieth birthday which is described as 'a very careful piece in which Hoskyns picked out what he appreciated in Barth and was silent about much else'.[31] Above all Hoskyns is grateful to Barth for his description of theology as '*ministerium verbi divini*',[32] which is a reminder to many 'that their theological and ministerial work should be of a properly scriptural quality and temper, and that their business is, as Pusey once told the Church of England, to set forth the meaning of Holy Scripture itself, to "extract" truth from, not to "import" truths into it. There are some also who owe to you the power of speech, the recognition that their work must be accompanied by that utterance in word or writing and action which is rid of every desire for personal notoriety or for the triumph of a school of thought. . . .'[33]

It might be said that the first part of Hoskyns' commentary on John presents something of a 'mix', and this 'mix' would seem to be the result of a combination of three major ingredients: Cambridge critical scholarship, traditional Anglican theology with its patristic basis, and Barthian transcendental philosophy of religion. This can be illustrated by reference to the section 2:23–3:21, on Jesus and Nicodemus the Rabbi. As it now stands this section contains an introduction, the text reproduced from the Revised Version, an extended comment and then what is called 'commentary'. It is this section of commentary which retains the greatest link with the later unrevised sections; and those, with the earlier articles, clearly have their origin in what can be called 'Cambridge critical scholarship'. The reader is given information on the major words, and frequent reference is made to other parts of scripture. Nicodemus, for example, is said to be a fairly common Greek name, transliterated into Hebrew as Naqdemon, and 'it is probable that the Evangelist intends to suggest, at least to his Jewish readers, that he was a member of the wealthy, aristocratic, and distinguished family which had furnished Aristobulus with his ambassador to Pompey in 63 B.C. . . .'[34] In the comment on those 'born of water and the Spirit [entering] into the Kingdom of God', Hoskyns illustrates how 'the Evangelist here and elsewhere (1.13, I John 2:29, 3:9, 4:7, 5:1) assumes that his readers are familiar with the description of baptism and conversion in terms of generation (I Pet. 1:3, 22–3, 2:2, 3:18–22; Jas. 1:18; Titus 3:5) or of creation (Rom. 6:1–2, I Cor. 3:1–2, II Cor. 5:17, Gal. 4:4–6 and 6:15, cf. Rom. 12:2, Eph. 4:22–4, Col. 3:9–10, Heb. 5:12–14).'[35] Numerous references to scripture are accompanied by references to other scholars whose work formed an important constituent in 'Cambridge critical scholarship'. Thus reference is made in this section to Bauer, Schlatter, Reitzenstein, Bernard and Westcott among others, to show either agreement or disagreement with the author's own point of view. This has to be set within the context of Hoskyns' own survey of Johannine scholarship, which is to be found as a chapter in the introduction entitled 'The Controversy'. This survey, which one reviewer regarded as 'perhaps the most original and the best feature of the work',[36] illustrates Hoskyns' wide knowledge of both British and continental scholarship and his judgement on it and on the issues it raised for the commentator. Hoskyns is critical of critical orthodoxy — where such scholars as Holtzmann and Loisy regarded John as 'the first and greatest of Christian mystics'[37] and his purpose as being that of attempting to 'plant Christianity in the Greek world and make of it the universal religion'.[38] He is critical too of traditional orthodoxy — of such conservative scholars as Lagrange who treated John 'primarily as a record of the events of the ministry of Jesus to which the Evangelist bears authentic witness'.[39] He considered English Johannine scholarship, compared with that of the continent, to be 'insular, provincial, traditional, Patristic, and apologetic'.[40] Westcott and Scott Holland, however, stand apart from this because of their brilliance and their historical and theological competence. They 'stood near the Evangelist because their critical and historical work also revolved round' the same theological concentration which revealed the Truth that the divine factor lies behind christological understanding and, indeed, behind the whole of life. This was also the Fourth Evangelist's desire, and in their attempt to interpret him their work 'was not permitted to be detached in its technical historical learning and erudition. For this reason [it] deserves to be remembered at a time when we are struggling back with great difficulty to a theological interpretation of the gospels.'[41]

Although this 'commentary' on 2:23–3:21 resembles the earlier unrevised sections, frequent references are now made to Schlatter's *Der Evangelist Johannes*.[42] Published in 1930, this maintained a strongly Jewish and Rabbinic background for the Fourth Gospel and the heavy underlining in the first six chapters of Hoskyns' copy of Schlatter testify to how sympathetic he found it. This was partly because it confirmed his own view that the Fourth Gospel must be placed firmly within the biblical and Christian tradition. In his introduction to the Nicodemus section, this point is emphasised: if the reader is to understand Johannine discourses 'he must understand them in their scriptural setting. Unless he is to do grave violence to the text, he is not free to put them in any other setting, ancient or modern. The Fourth Gospel is a biblical book, and the first discourse is spoken to a Jewish Rabbi . . . each discourse moves step by step as an ordered, theologically ordered, whole: until, that is to say, what is said becomes intelligible and coherent speech, and until, moreover, it coheres with the biblical Palestinian background upon which the Evangelist has set it, even though he be writing in Greek, years after the Temple was destroyed and when the Jews no longer congregated in Jerusalem.'[43] This picks up what had already been said in the Introduction, which does not deal with such matters as authorship and the date and place of writing, but with the theological problems related to the Fourth Gospel and its authority. Thus no information is given, or can be given, about the church which first received the Nicodemus discourse, and which would have found it relevant, because 'the author has done his best, apparently with intention, to cover up his tracks. For his theme is not his own workshop but the workshop of God, and to this we have no direct access!'[44] The Fourth Gospel is said to be 'a rest-less book',[45] this being 'not because, owing to some lack of knowledge which further patient study may, and surely will, rectify, the critic has just failed to reach an adequate solution of the problem, but because the theme of the book is beyond human knowledge, and because if it did come to rest, it would have denied the theme, which, in fact, it never denies.'[46]

Yet although it is said that this author did his best 'to cover up his tracks' and produced 'a rest-less book', this is certainly not to say that he produced a disordered book. In fact his aim was precisely the opposite. Hoskyns believes that, like Ignatius, John was confronted with a disorderly historical tradition and church life; and that he collected together fragments of a tradition which was in danger of being distorted and produced a Gospel which 'moves on spirally'.[47] (By this obscure phrase Hoskyns meant that the story, as told by John, is like a spire. It begins with the broad base of Jesus' ministry to the crowds, narrowing from chapter 13 with discourses to the disciples, and reaching a focal point with the death of Jesus.) He is also convinced that John knew Mark and that Mark acted as his primary source for his knowledge of the life and death of Jesus, but 'it is surely quite clear that the author of the Fourth Gospel is not content to leave this knowledge in the form in which it was already possessed by his readers. His book must have been a disturbing book.'[48] Part of this disturbance, as can be illustrated by the Nicodemus discourse, is caused by the fact that this author has allowed some of the themes that he treats in common with Mark (e.g. obedience, prayer and persecution) to move into the centre of his theological structure, and to be written up in the form of extended discourse rather than short episodic units. The author, however, is not to be regarded as one who merely records mystical experience, because he repeatedly emphasises the central importance of historicity, 'the flesh of Jesus the Son of man'. Thus the Gospel contains both history and interpretation, but to separate them is an impossible task. 'In other words, the theme of the Fourth Gospel is the non-historical that makes sense of history, the infinite that makes sense of time, God who makes sense of men and is therefore their Saviour. . . . The non-historical factor penetrates our supposed historical data and the historical factor is woven into what is manifestly non-historical. Moreover, the non-historical cannot be dismissed as Johannine interpretation.'[49] In spite of the impossibility of separating history and interpretation, Hoskyns places the Nicodemus discourse against its biblical and Palestinian background and shows that the author has constructed the discourse as a theologically ordered whole. Thus far he has been true to 'Cambridge critical scholarship', but this gives place to 'Barthian exegesis' in the introductory exposition where the biblical references largely disappear and the discourse is treated thematically.

In this introductory exposition four themes are discerned: (1) repentance; (2) Jesus himself, the visible, historical man; (3) the Death of the Son of man and the Love of God; and (4) judgement and salvation, works and faith. Regarding repentance, Hoskyns argues that Nicodemus, being a materialist, did not understand that the knowledge of God is not achieved by the acquisition of more information but by a new, creative beginning. Nicodemus' failure to perceive this was 'not because he takes visible human life seriously, but because he does not see what it means: he does not see that human birth is itself speaking of that which lies beyond it and above it; it is speaking of the creative act of God, of birth from above.'[50] This supernatural birth, however, is only intelligible to those who are born of the Spirit. 'There is no evolution from flesh to Spirit. What a man is in his own eyes or in the eyes of his religious companions is at best a parable of what he is as the creation of

God: at worst it is a darkness from which he must escape at all costs.'[51] But (the second theme) it is Jesus himself who is the means by which this creative new birth can take place, as the 'firm earth is the place where God wills to reveal Himself . . . Though no man has ascended into heaven, yet God has willed that there should be a descent from heaven to earth; not an apparition or epiphany in the sky, but a real descent into human flesh. This descent is the mission of Jesus; and now at last the prophetic phrase son of man has received its true historical meaning.'[52] But (in the third theme) the discourse moves straight to the death of this Son of man because 'the place of death is the place of revelation', and this revelation is of the love of God. 'For this reason, the road to death, the death of the son of man, is the determined direction of the mission of the Son of God, determined, not by fate nor by mischance nor by the will of His enemies, but by the love of God for men.'[53] Finally (the fourth theme) Nicodemus is therefore confronted with the possibilities of faith or of unbelief. 'Faith is not a separable fragment of human behaviour, nor is unbelief a detachable thing done in the midst of other things. Faith is not a wish that remains unfulfilled, nor is unbelief the refusal to stretch out towards some distant goal. To believe is to apprehend human action, all human action, in its relation to God; not to believe is not to recognize the only context in which human behaviour can be anything more than trivial. The man who believes apprehends that every visible human act requires to be fulfilled by the invisible, creative action of God. The man who believes recognizes that all human behaviour is by itself and in itself incomplete. The man who believes knows that God fills up this incompleteness, and that in filling it up, he makes of the human act a thing that is wrought in God. This is the love of God . . . But the generality of men hate this exposure of their behaviour. They will not face the pain of it. They do not think that their actions require to be fulfilled, for their affections are set upon themselves . . . These men are atheists: they remain in the darkness, and their whole behaviour is evil. They stand under the majestic judgement of God. This is the issue raised by the historical figure of Jesus, by His words and actions and finally by His death.'[54]

Hoskyns' deference to patristic exegesis is seen especially in his analysis of John 6. In his note on 'The Interpretation of the Sixth Chapter', which he felt it necessary to add, he identifies three main lines of interpretation.[55] First, the language is metaphorical throughout; what is eaten and drunk are the Lord's words, and if the Evangelist had the Eucharist in mind at all he has completely spiritualised it. Some of the

Reformers (Calvin is quoted) took this view when they applied the eating and drinking to the assimilation by faith of the benefits of Christ's sacrifice. Secondly, although the language of vv. 51–58 might be regarded as sacramental, they stand in contradiction to the rest of the discourse which is not. These verses are therefore a later addition and their presence is due to ecclesiastical redaction. Thirdly, the discourse is homogeneous and is sacrificial and sacramental throughout, but that is because in it the Christian religion has been assimilated to non-Jewish cults. Hoskyns himself dissents from all these views, because he sees the situation of the Evangelist as that of one who is faced on the one hand by a misunderstanding of the gospel of the historical existence of Christ as crude materialism, and on the other hand by an anti-sacramental movement of pure Spirit within Christianity. Thus he regards patristic exegesis as more correct than modern exegesis, because the Fathers tended not to refer the language of the chapter exclusively either to feeding on the words of Jesus or to the sacrament. He quotes from Clement of Alexandria, Eusebius and Augustine; Augustine he finds particularly significant because 'while applying the Flesh of the Lord to the Church, he adds at once that the sacrament of the unity of the Body and Blood of Christ "is prepared on the Lord's table in some places daily . . ."; and in another passage speaks of the command to "eat the Flesh of the Son of man" as a figure of enjoining that we should share in the sufferings of our Lord, and that we should retain a "sweet and profitable memory of the fact that His flesh was wounded and crucified for us".'[56] Hoskyns' own comment on the chapter follows from this: '*The living Bread* or *Flesh* is to the author of the gospel a comprehensive symbolical phrase containing a whole series of suggestions. It is to him what *Corpus Christi* is to a Catholic Christian. Fundamentally it suggests the Christ incarnate, offered as a sacrifice, and finally glorified. It is then extended to embrace the regenerate believers who have been saved by the Christ. They are the true and living Bread which must not and indeed cannot be lost. These suggestions are all focussed in the Eucharist, which is not considered as a rite isolated or detached from Christian faith as a whole, but as the concretion of the Christ incarnate, sacrificed and glorified for the nourishment of the faithful.'[57]

What then is to be made of this 'mix'? R.H. Fuller, in a description of Hoskyns' commentary, notes a remark of E. Käsemann that this commentary is 'the only really Barthian commentary on the fourth Gospel, comparable to Barth's own commentary on the Epistle to the Romans in scope, style and import'.[58] C.K. Barrett also takes up this point, stating his belief that 'this is not far from the truth.'[59] In the eyes of at least one reviewer, writing when the commentary was first published, this was an adverse development. 'When Hoskyns was in the process of writing this commentary he fell under the spell of Karl Barth, in whom he saw a champion of the Theological as against the Higher Critical School of Biblical interpreters, and through whose influence he abandoned his earlier Liberal Catholic apologetic. The parts of the Commentary, which the writer was able to revise before his death, both in style and subjectmatter reflect in particular the Barthian influence. The treatment of the eschatology, the interpretation of the Logos, and the love of unintelligible paradox are all illustrations . . . The attempt is not satisfactory and reveals, I think, one of the weak points in Hoskyns' method of working.'[60]

But are these statements a fair assessment of the 'mix'? It should be noted at the outset that a number of different points are being made. It is one thing to compare the effect that each of the two commentaries made in their respective situations, but it is another to say that Hoskyns' John is similar in 'scope, style and import' to Barth's Romans; and it is yet another to say that Hoskyns' John is a 'Barthian commentary'. And all these comments fail to take account of the 'mix'. Barth's Romans was published after the holocaust of a world war and clearly had enormous effect upon continental theology, while Hoskyns' John had a more diffuse effect and perhaps has 'never found the recognition it deserves'.[61] What then can be made of the remark that the commentary is similar in 'scope, style and import' to Barth's Romans? Clearly this is an over-generalised statement, as even a cursory glance at the commentaries will show. Even in the revised sections of his John, Hoskyns has retained the 'unrevised' section which he calls 'commentary', and which gives details concerning the major words and their biblical background which Barth does not give. For example, Hoskyns gives much biblical detail about the expression 'the Kingdom of God' (John 3:3) whereas Barth gives no such detail about 'the righteousness of God' (Romans 1:16). It is unfair to say that through Barth's influence Hoskyns has 'abandoned his earlier Liberal Catholic apologetic',[62] because although he wrote a revised essay to accompany each section, he retained his earlier commentary. Thus even in the revised section up to 6:31 the new additional essays and the earlier commentary are designed to be read together. It is therefore not a case of abandoning an earlier method of working and replacing it with a new method, but of adding to and 'improving' on what was already there. This can be clearly illustrated from the Nicodemus passage already cited. Here, even given Hoskyns' 'revised' layout, there are notable similarities with one of his earliest pieces of theological writing where he deals with John 3:1–21.[63] The section in his *The Fourth Gospel* on Nicodemus marked 'commentary' is similar to what he wrote earlier, the main words and theological ideas being set out. Then in the article there follows what he calls 'interpretation', which explains the sequence of thought of the passage. What then has happened between the composition of the article and the revision of the commentary? First, Hoskyns has reversed the order. Here interpretation now comes first, followed by commentary. The commentary is also now more complicated, frequent references being made to Schlatter, which has the effect of intensifying Hoskyns' view that the Fourth Gospel should be primarily understood as a biblical book, rooted in biblical tradition. An example of an 'enlarged' rather than a 'changed' comment can be seen with reference to 3:17, where the Son is said to be sent into the world by God for salvation rather than for judgement. In the article Hoskyns notes that 'separation and judgement follow naturally as men believe or disbelieve in the name of the only begotten Son of God. But the object of the coming of the Son is not primarily judgement, but salvation. The judgement in the present does not exclude the final judgement (5:28, 12:48).'[64] In the commentary Hoskyns declares that 'the divine purpose of the mission of Jesus is, therefore, salvation not judgement, eternal life and not destruction or corruption (Luke 19:10). Since, however, the mission of Jesus — and pre-eminently the manner of His death — bring out into the open the radical distinction between those who believe and those who do not (1 John 4:2,3) the theme of judgement persists throughout the Fourth Gospel.[. . .] The Greek verb to judge and the corresponding noun judgement mean first the act of separating or distinguishing and then the consequent act of pronouncing upon what has been separated.'[65] Yet these two statements are not different in essence. In the second, the comments about judgement are an 'enlarged' form of what is possible in a short article, and here judgement is linked with the manner of Jesus' death; and the difference this implies for believers and unbelievers is made more absolute. Even the earlier articles contain what might be supposed to be 'Barthian' comments ('obliterate the otherworldliness of Christianity, and it ceases to be religion') written before Hoskyns had read Barth.

It is thus in the 'interpretative' sections that the biggest changes can be detected. In the article Hoskyns illustrates how John used the Nicodemus incident 'to show what claims Christianity has upon educated Jews, who were attracted by the new religion, but feared excommunication from the synagogue, and to impress upon Christians the real meaning of their baptism.'[66] This is a study of the passage as it stands with no attempt to relate it to modern thought. With the interpretative section in the commentary, however, this situation has changed. Hoskyns now speaks of Nicodemus as 'materialistic',[67] and takes him as an illustration of the fact that 'theologians were led to poise themselves in mid-air, lose their balance, and forfeit their right to exist.'[68] The light of Jesus is said to penetrate 'every corner of human behaviour, and either lights it up or throws it into the darkness. There is no twilight in His presence, for he compels the final distinction between those who have everlasting life and those who have lost everything (vv. 15–16).'[69] These statements are attempts to apply the teaching of the Fourth Gospel to the contemporary situation. They are what would today be termed 'hermeneutic'. It was Barth's aim in the composition of his Romans to make the voice of Paul speak clearly to his generation, and it is probably this that Hoskyns learnt from him, and which he put into practice when he 'revised' his John. However, this was not new for Hoskyns, and can be detected, as has been already indicated, in some of his 'Cambridge Sermons'. What Barth did for Hoskyns was to bring about a sharpening of his theological activity, and suggest ways in which this could be expressed. C.K. Barrett believes that 'the comparison between Barth and Hoskyns brings to mind Barth's own description of Calvin and Calvin's commentaries: 'How energetically Calvin, having first established what stands in the text, sets himself to re-think the whole material and to wrestle with it, till the walls which separate the sixteenth century from the first become transparent! Paul speaks, and the man of the sixteenth century hears.' That is surely the goal that Hoskyns sets for himself.[70]

Yet to call the commentary 'Barthian' on this basis is to be one-sided. For example, in his note on 'The Interpretation of the Sixth Chapter' Hoskyns rejects Calvin's view that this chapter is to be interpreted in terms of assimilating by faith the benefits of Christ's atoning sacrifice, and instead opts for the view taken by the Fathers.[71] And the numerous references in the commentary to the Fathers illustrates how highly Hoskyns prized their commentaries and exegesis; it was also valued in Anglican Catholic apologetic, particularly since Keble. In discussing 1:13 and 14, Hoskyns notes that the question arises whether or not the language here presupposes the Virgin Birth.[72] He then quotes Ignatius, Justin, Irenaeus, Augustine and the author of the *Epistola Apostolorum*, all of whom refer to the Virgin Birth in language which recalls that of the prologue. Even though it is most likely that the plural 'were born' of v. 13 is to be accepted as original, it is still probable that this was intended to convey an allusion to the birth of Christ.[73] It must remain a matter of speculation whether Hoskyns would have seen fit to revise his previous comment on the incident at the foot of the cross between Jesus' mother and the beloved disciple: 'At the time of the Lord's death a new family is brought into being. If the unity of the Church is symbolized by the seamless robe, the peculiar nature of that unity is indicated here. The Church proceeds from the sacrifice of the Son of God, and the union of the Beloved Disciple and the Mother of the Lord prefigures and foreshadows the charity of the Ecclesia of God. Mary, the Mother of the Lord, becomes the mother of the faithful [here Hoskyns refers to his earlier article, 'Genesis I–III and St. John's Gospel', *J.T.S.*, April 1920, pp. 210ff], and the Beloved Disciple here seems to denote the ideal Christian convert.'[74] Here at least, Liberal Catholic apologetic relating to the Church and Mary is still strong, and there seems no reason to suppose, bearing in mind what Hoskyns said about the Virgin Birth in 1:13, that it would have been abandoned at a later time.

Throughout the different levels of the commentary one particular conviction and emphasis remains paramount, viz. that the Fourth Gospel must be understood as essentially a biblical book, 'a book which stands within the biblical tradition and requires for its understanding those same presuppositions one discovers in the reading of Isaiah, Mark, Romans, and the like.'[75] In an early article Hoskyns had maintained that the starting point for understanding the Johannine prologue is the opening chapters of Genesis, because John saw Christianity 'as the new creation, and the return to the presence of God, which had been lost by the sin of Adam and Eve . . . Such a creative act can only be explained by the claim that Jesus was the incarnate Word of God.'[76] In his commentary Hoskyns reinforces this Christological dimension. 'The texture of the prologue is taken from the Old Testament Scriptures (e.g. Gen. i, Prov. viii); but it is altogether Christian. That Jesus once spoke is more fundamental for its understanding than is the history of Greek philosophy or the story of the westward progress of Oriental mysticism; more fundamental even than the first chapter of Genesis or the eighth chapter of the Proverbs.'[77] This is also applied to the whole Gospel, when it is said that 'the workshop in which the Word of God was forged to take its natural place among the great theological descriptions of Jesus and His work is a Christian workshop: the tools are Christian tools.'[78] But it must be asked if this suffices as it stands for an adequate treatment of the Gospel. Barrett suggests that Hoskyns did not fully attain the goal that he set for himself because 'his methods were not radical enough. . . . It seems to me that we, just when we study and observe these "other spirits" as they pass through the hands of an author, come to know not only the personal faith of the author, but also the creative power of the New Testament. . . . It is precisely Hoskyns' failure to undertake this analytical task that is the greatest weakness of his commentary.'[79] This is indeed a fundamental weakness of the commentary which Barrett has noted, namely its supposition that when a thoroughly 'biblical' exegesis is reached, then it can be claimed that the commentator has arrived at the authentic word of God. Although it may be partly true that the Fourth Gospel is 'strictly related to the heart of Judaism', this can never be said to be the whole truth because 'Judaism' itself cannot be understood as a single entity; there were Palestinian, Hellenistic, Alexandrian and Sectarian forms of Judaism. Judaism, being a highly complex phenomenon by the time the Fourth Gospel was written, needs to be carefully analysed if it is to be of any value in determining the background of a biblical book. However, the exegesis of John demands an investigation of 'other spirits', Hellenism and Gnosticism. Hoskyns had already admitted that the author has done his best 'to cover up his tracks', so that it is difficult to discover from the Gospel as it stands where it ought to be placed on the 'thought-map' of early Christianity. If the author has any contact at all with the Ancient world outside Palestine, it is necessary to take account of that world in which he lived and worked. The author of the Fourth Gospel is too elusive a writer to be tied down to any particular background.

In Hoskyns' attempt at 'Johannine hermeneutic' we have found an essaying of a personal statement of theology similar to that given by Barth in his commentary on Romans. However, although Cranfield believes that that commentary marks a turning-point in the history of theology, he also maintains that 'it has very serious deficiencies as an exposition of Romans.'[80] Could Hoskyns' commentary on John be said, for the same reasons, to have 'very serious deficiencies as an exposition' of John? Is it a possible, or even a desirable exercise to attempt to break down the walls between this century and the one in which John wrote? Has Hoskyns' hermeneutical task been successful? Hoskyns doubtless saw, as Barth saw, that biblical books, especially New Testament books, should be commented upon in such a way as both to reveal their theological treasures and to 'speak' to modern humanity in whatever condition it finds itself, especially that of tragedy and purposelessness. In the end it must be left to individual judgement to decide whether Hoskyns' attempt at this in his revision of his commentary on John has been true to the intentions of that author and, at the same time, has made the words of the Gospel relevant to the human condition.

NOTES

1. E.C. Hoskyns, 'Genesis I–III and St. John's Gospel', *J.T.S.*, XXI. 1920, p. 210.
2. ibid., p. 211.
3. ibid., p. 212.
4. ibid., p. 213.
5. ibid., p. 215.
6. ibid., p. 217.
7. ibid., p. 218.
8. E.C. Hoskyns, 'Adversaria Exegetica: St. John III. 1–21', *Theology*, I, 1920, p. 86.
9. ibid., p. 87.
10. ibid.
11. ibid., p. 89.
12. E.C. Hoskyns, 'Adversaria Exegetica: St. John II. 13–22: The Old and the New Worship of God', *Theology*, I, 1920, p. 146.
13. ibid.
14. E.C. Hoskyns, 'Adversaria Exegetica: St. John X, 1–18: The Good Shepherd', *Theology* II, 1921, p. 206.
15. ibid., p. 207.
16. E.C. Hoskyns, *The Fourth Gospel*, ed. F.N. Davey, London, 1940, revised 1-vol. edn, 1947. All references are to this latter edition, this particular one from p. 7.
17. *20th Century Defenders*, p. 90.
18. *Cambridge Sermons*, p. ix.
19. Neill, op. cit., p. 214.
20. Quoted by J. McConnachie, *The Significance of Karl Barth*, London, 1931, p. 43.
21. K. Barth, *The Epistle to the Romans*, Eng. transl. E.C. Hoskyns, Oxford, 1933, pp. 331f.
22. *Cambridge Sermons*, pp. 119f.
23. *Cambridge Sermons*, pp. 147f.
24. ibid., p. 91.
25. ibid., p. 121.

26. ibid., p. 35.
27. ibid., p. 77 and 80f.
28. *J.T.S.*, XXXIII, 1932, p. 205.
29. Jacques Maritain (1882–1973) was a French Thomist philosopher who was converted to Roman Catholicism in 1906. Subsequently he was professor at Paris, Toronto and Princeton. He endeavoured to apply the Classical doctrines of Thomism to metaphysics, to moral and social philosophy, and to the philosophy of education, history and culture. He also discussed the relation of philosophy to religious experience, and it was in this area that his ideas were close to those of Barth.
30. *J.T.S.*, XXIX, 1928, p. 204.
31. *Cambridge Sermons*, p. xxvii.
32. ibid., p. 219. This letter first appeared in *Theologische Aufsätze: Karl Barth zum 50*, Munich, 1936, pp. 525–7.
33. ibid., p. 221.
34. *The Fourth Gospel*, p. 210.
35. ibid., p. 214.
36. Review by R.V.G. Tasker, *C.Q.R.*, CXXX, 1940, p. 319.
37. *The Fourth Gospel*, p. 22.
38. ibid., p. 23.
39. ibid., p. 27.
40. ibid., p. 35.
41. ibid., p. 47.
42. Adolf Schlatter (1852–1938) spent most of his academic career in Tübingen. There he declared that the Bible was to be treated as a coherent whole and ought to be understood as a unity amidst differences, because it speaks of a history of revelation and faith, brought about by God, which has its unity and its central point in Christ. More details can be found in an article by P. Stuhlmacher, 'Adolf Schlatter's Interpretation of Scripture', *N.T.S.*, 24, 1978, pp. 433–46. Schlatter produced many detailed commentaries on most NT books (p. 438), and Stuhlmacher believes that Schlatter prepared for the counterblast against 'theological liberalism' before Barth (p. 440). He was a friend and colleague of G. Kittel. Certainly parallels can be made between Schlatter and Hoskyns; both, for example, viewed the Bible as a whole and both were accused of being 'uncritical'.
43. *The Fourth Gospel*, p. 201.
44. ibid., pp. 18f.
45. ibid., p. 19.
46. ibid., p. 20.
47. ibid., p. 67.
48. ibid., p. 73.
49. ibid., pp. 129f.
50. ibid., p. 203.

51. ibid., p. 204.
52. ibid., p. 205.
53. ibid., p. 206.
54. ibid., p. 208.
55. ibid., pp. 304–7.
56. ibid., p. 306.
57. ibid., p. 305.
58. R.H. Fuller, *The New Testament in Current Study*, London, 1963, p. 117.
59. C.K. Barrett, *The Gospel of John and Judaism*, London, 1975, p. 5.
60. Review by R.V.G. Tasker, *C.Q.R.*, CXXX, 1940, p. 320.
61. Barrett, op. cit., p. 5.
62. Tasker, op. cit., p. 320. Note also a comment by J.M. Creed, *J.T.S.*, XL, 1939, p. 210: 'For though he became saturated with the prophetic style of the *Römerbrief* and in a measure came to use it himself, he in no way weakened in his loyalty to the tradition of High Anglicanism.'
63. 'Adversaria Exegetica: St. John III. 1–21', *Theology*, I, Aug. 1920, pp. 83–9.
64. ibid., p. 86.
65. *The Fourth Gospel*, pp. 218f.
66. 'Adversaria Exegetica: St. John III. 1–21', pp. 87f.
67. *The Fourth Gospel*, p. 203.
68. ibid., p. 205.
69. ibid., p. 209.
70. Barrett, op. cit., p. 5.
71. *The Fourth Gospel*, p. 304.
72. ibid., pp. 164f.
73. ibid., p. 166. See also M.F. Wiles, *The Spiritual Gospel: The Interpretation of the Fourth Gospel in the Early Church*, Cambridge, 1960, p. 106.
74. *The Fourth Gospel*, p. 530.
75. Barrett, op. cit., p. 5.
76. 'Genesis I–III and St. John's Gospel', p. 217.
77. *The Fourth Gospel*, p. 137.
78. ibid., p. 162.
79. Barrett, op. cit., pp. 5f.
80. C.E.B. Cranfield, *A Critical and Exegetical Commentary on the Epistle to the Romans*, vol. 1, Edinburgh, 1975, p. 42.

6

ST JOHN II

In this concluding chapter some attempt will be made to explore further the character and validity of Hoskyns' work on the Fourth Gospel by considering it in relation to the work of subsequent writers on that Gospel and their attitude to and use of Hoskyns, whether they reproduced his positions or carried them further, or called them into question.

Fundamental to Hoskyns' approach was that the Fourth Gospel was what he called a 'biblical' book standing within the 'biblical tradition', and that it represented what he calls 'apostolic Christianity'. He nowhere explicitly defines these terms, but takes them for granted as a basis, and allows their meaning to be established in the course of interpreting John's text. They presuppose a theological unity of the New Testament, indeed of the whole Bible, and an assumption that Christianity developed with a comparative uniformity which could be called 'apostolic'. Hoskyns was not unaware that a non-biblical Hellenistic background had been postulated for John's Gospel. This can be seen by the number of times he refers to the commentary of Walter Bauer, who was a representative of 'the History of Religion School'. He was convinced, however, that this approach was mistaken and he set out to refute it. The most extreme example of this approach is now Bultmann's commentary,[1] which could be said to be a monument to it. In the footnotes to his commentary and in his introduction to individual sections, Bultmann made considerable use of 'parallels' from Gnostic sources in order to set out his view that much of the Johannine discourse material originates in a non-biblical setting. Thus in the image of the Good Shepherd in chapter 10 Bultmann saw great differences from the Old Testament, especially in the reciprocal relationship of shepherd and sheep; these show 'that the Johannine shepherd is either an original conception, or else that it stands in another tradition.'[2] Bultmann argued the latter, maintaining that 'it is probable that the image of the shepherd was taken from the Gnostic tradition, like the images in the rest of the revelation-discourses.'[3] These discourses would thus hardly be Christian at all but of Gnostic origin and content, finding their way into the Evangelist's hands through the Baptist sect. This thesis is central to Bultmann's approach and underlines much of his exegesis, since he believed that the key to the Evangelist's thinking lies in the way that he uses and modifies the Gnostic source material which he has received so that it can be applicable to Jesus who, as the man from Heaven, defines the true nature of existence and the means of entering into it.

Much of this Hoskyns would clearly have found deeply mistaken, for it countered his view that 'it is almost impossible to escape from the conviction that the reader of the Gospel is at the very heart of Apostolic Christianity.'[4] Bultmann's thesis about the sources of the Fourth Gospel suffers because these sources are difficult to detect and the thesis is thus difficult to prove. In assigning much of the Evangelist's theological material to a Gnostic background which is hard to trace, and in not including material in his commentary concerning the Church and the nature of 'apostolic' Christianity, Bultmann tends to leave the Fourth Gospel hanging in the air. For Hoskyns, 'in the First Epistle of John, which must be assumed to have come from the same hand as the gospel, a somewhat stronger light is thrown upon the readers of the epistle and, therefore, presumably, upon the original readers of the gospel also.'[5] Ironically, although he wrote a commentary on the Johannine Epistles in the Meyer series, Bultmann does not use I John for this purpose or for purposes of theology, but only on matters of style and to illustrate how the author has constructed a prose redaction from a rhythmical source. Bultmann also severed the link between the Fourth Gospel and the synoptic tradition by, for example, assigning many of the 'Father-Son' sayings to his non-Christian source, implying that this was their theological origin.[6] Hoskyns, on the other hand, saw their origin in the Marcan record of the divine voice at the Baptism of Jesus and at his Transfiguration.[7] A more moderate version of Bultmann's approach, and one nearer home, was that of C.H. Dodd,[8] who gave considerable attention to the Hermetic literature[9] in his investigation of the thought background of the Gospel. 'It remains true', comments Dodd in a review of Hoskyns' work, 'that converts from the "higher paganism" recognized that the Fourth Gospel spoke largely the language with which they were familiar, and that it especially interested those Gnostics who tried to combine Christianity with non-Christian ideas . . . The Word was made flesh: the scandalous character of that statement (to use a favourite expression of Hoskyns) is never so emphatic as when it is read after a study of some of the purest religious teaching which has come down to us from the non-Christian world of that time.'[10] Dodd believed, then, that the most significant parallels to the Fourth Gospel are to be found in Philo and in the Hermetic literature. He used these parallels, which often state the very opposite of what John says, to establish the most important Christian characteristics of the Gospel. 'What has been said of one libellus may be said also of the whole body of Hermetic writings. It seems clear that as a whole they represent a type of religious thought akin to one side of Johannine thought, without any substantial borrowing on the one part or the other.'[11] Furthermore, he maintains that the background of the Gospel pre-supposes 'a range of ideas having a remarkable resemblance to those of Hellenistic Judaism as represented by Philo'.[12] These led Dodd to the conclusion that 'it seems therefore that we are to think of the work as addressed to a wide public consisting primarily of devout and thoughtful persons . . . in the varied and cosmopolitan society of a great Hellenistic city such as Ephesus under the Roman Empire.'[13]

In a review of *The Interpretation of the Fourth Gospel*, important because it gives insight into what Hoskyns might have thought of the book,[14] Davey finds himself 'in grateful and considerable agreement'. This 'is certain to clarify and stimulate further study of theology, not only of the Fourth Gospel but also of the Primitive Church, for many years to come.'[15] However, he has misgivings about certain points in Dodd's interpretation and about implications in some of his conclusions. Davey doubts if the Fourth Gospel is addressed to two different classes of reader as Dodd appears to suggest. 'Dr Dodd observes, from time to time, details that may substantiate his assumption that this Gospel is addressed to non-Christian readers. Yet it is also part of his thesis that what the evangelist writes is also intended to be understood at a level too deep for these non-Christian readers . . . Could such a carefully and successfully integrated work as the Fourth Gospel really have been composed as at one and the same time an apology to non-Christians and a deepening and recasting of the Gospel for Christians?'[16] As for Dodd's use of the Hermetic literature, Davey asks if this has led him 'not only to adopt a too particularized definition of the evangelist's intentions, but to ascribe to the evangelist a too technically informed Platonic dialectic.'[17] Here Davey repeats Hoskyns' claim that the real clue to understanding the Fourth Gospel is to be found within the biblical and Christian tradition and that the precise background against which the gospel was written, especially in relation to the pagan world, is now too difficult to uncover.[18]

As one particular constituent of what he called the biblical tradition, Hoskyns refers again and again to apostolic Christianity as the matrix of the Fourth Gospel and as governing the particular form of Christian tradition which it represents. The 'apostolic foundation of the Church conditions the movement and "lay-out" of the gospel; its horizon narrowing until Jesus, after the final rejection by the Jewish authorities and by the crowds, is depicted alone with His disciples, entrusting to them His authoritative mission to the world in the power of the Holy Spirit of Truth (chs 13–17, 20: 22, 23). Only after this severe concentration does the author of the Fourth Gospel permit his readers to occupy their proper position as fish caught by apostolic fishermen and as sheep under the care of an apostolic shepherd.'[19] This later generation had been 'so completely created by apostolic witness and formed by apostolic obedience that they are veritably carried across into the company of the original disciples of Jesus and invested with the authority of their mission.'[20] The author of the Fourth Gospel also saw in the life of Jesus 'the glory of God making sense of the history, for it is the Spirit who giveth life — by itself the flesh is meaningless and unprofitable. This is not metaphysics, though it is what the proper metaphysician is in the end talking about. Rather this is apostolic Christianity, the rough material from which a philosophy may perhaps spring. This is the truth as it was seen by the Apostles of the Lord, by those who had been called into the theological tension of human life at its most acute point, at the place where Christ was crucified.'[21]

It is possible to be caught in a vicious circle, since the form which Christianity took in any one area depends on the interpretation put upon the various books of the New Testament; or, as F.G. Downing has maintained, a quest of the primitive Church is just as necessary as a quest of the historical Jesus.[22] This is illustrated by Ernst Käsemann's book *The Testament of Jesus* which, although it clearly regards Hoskyns' commentary as a major contribution to Johannine studies, arrives at precisely the opposite conclusion: that the Fourth Gospel stands apart from apostolic Christianity, at least as Käsemann understands that term. He believes that this Gospel 'would fit best into a side tributary apart from the general stream yet connected with it.'[23] Furthermore, it does not fit well into the developing progress towards the formation of the Catholic Church, being first discovered and used by the Gnostics; 'the reason for this may be that John is the relic of a Christian conventicle existing on, or being pushed to, the Church's periphery.'[24] This conventicle he believed to be situated not too far from Palestine, possibly in Syria, and its presence there was to be welcomed, because 'sectarians also participated in the formation of the early Catholic Church and they were more influential than orthodoxy was at any time willing to admit.'[25] Yet it may be asked if Käsemann has not overstated the difference between 'orthodoxy' and 'heresy' at this early period in the Church's life, and misunderstood the relationship between apostolic authority and Catholic order. Hoskyns believed that the author of the Fourth Gospel wrote 'in order to check the disruptive tendencies in the Church of his day, created the notion of apostolic solidarity and of a united apostolic apprehension: and that therefore it was he who laid the foundations of the Church's teaching about the apostles, and indeed of its apostolic character.'[26] Hoskyns also argued that the situation lying behind Ignatius' epistles and the Fourth Gospel was similar and was evoked by similar if not identical circumstances, and that Ignatius saw the threefold ministry as the clue to Catholic order[27] while the author of the Fourth Gospel asked deeper questions about the nature of apostolic authority.[28] Because the Evangelist dealt with the matter in this way, rather than by stressing 'orders' like Ignatius, this did not, as Käsemann has suggested,[29] make him any less of a 'Catholic' author. It could be argued that the Fourth Gospel penetrated more deeply into the true nature of apostolic life in the Church than did Ignatius by concentrating on the ecclesiastical structures.

Yet lying behind 'apostolic Christianity', however understood, lies Christology. How the Evangelist understood the person of Christ is a key factor in the Fourth Gospel's presentation of Christianity. For St John any understanding of Christ is interwoven with his understanding of Christ's relationship to God and of the implications of this for apostolic authority: 'As the Father has sent me, so I send you.'[30] Hoskyns was clear that the author's purpose was theological. 'The theme of the Fourth Gospel is the non-historical that makes sense of history, the infinite that makes sense of time, God who makes sense of men and is therefore their Saviour.'[31] This is reinforced by Davey's essay: 'The truth made known in history is the truth of God: it is not, that is to say, the truth of observable history, but the truth of observable history in relation to Him whom no man hath seen at any time.'[32] Thus the Fourth Evangelist was concerned to confront his readers through Jesus with God and therefore, in the strictest sense of the term, his work can be deemed 'theological'.[33] Käsemann is critical of Hoskyns on this score,[34] maintaining that Christology was the Evangelist's main concern, his understanding here being docetic: 'One can hardly fail to recognize the danger of his [the Fourth Evangelist's] christology of glory, namely the danger of docetism. It is present in a still naive, unreflected form and it has not yet been recognized by the Evangelist or his community. . . .

We, too, have to give an answer to the question of the centre of the Christian message. From John we must learn that this is the question of the right Christology, and we have to recognize that he was able to give an answer only in the form of a naive docetism.'[35]

But is this how the Fourth Evangelist saw the matter? Whatever other purpose he may seem to have had, it was not to depict a God who only appeared as man. It may be the case that there is a measure of artificiality in his references to Jesus' weakness, weariness and 'ignorance' (the fact that during his incarnate life he did not have complete knowledge of everything), but this was because the author was attempting to say that Jesus was truly man. There is certainly no artificiality about his death: the Johannine Jesus shares fully with mankind in the universal human destiny, and frequently the glorification of Jesus is linked to the glory of his crucifixion. This Hoskyns understood well, as, for example, in his comment on 13: 31–33: 'Just as, in the earlier discourses, the theme *Jesus Himself*, Jesus in the flesh as the Revelation of God, has been followed and qualified by the theme *The Death of the Son of man and the love of God*, lest the glory of the Son of man should be thought to be an earthly glory and the Revelation of the glory of God should be misconstrued and obscured, so *now* the qualifying context of the Passion and Death makes possible direct speech about the glory of the Son of man (cf. 12:23–28). For the glory of the Son of man is the glory of the Father.'[36] This takes us into the heart of Johannine theology, as C.K. Barrett has observed: '. . . . it was not John's intention to write about a divine-human hybrid, but about a real man who was unique in that when men looked at him with the eye of faith they saw the invisible God.'[37] Yet, like any other theologian, the Fourth Evangelist had to wrestle with what this means. That is why he made two apparently contradictory statements about the same person: 'I and the Father are one' (10:30) and 'the Father is greater than I' (14:28). This was because he wished to make it clear 'that God in his revelation is truly God; that Jesus reveals not a secondary deity but the Most High God. Yet he is *Deus revelatus*; not the whole abyss of Godhead, but God known.'[38] Thus it must be made clear that from the beginning the Son was utterly dependent upon the Father. This is rigorously maintained throughout the Fourth Gospel (e.g. 4:34, 5:30, 6:38) together with the fact that the Son did not seek his own glory. The author was therefore 'careful to emphasize that Christianity is not an independent cult about Jesus, but the revelation of the Father and the worship of God. The Christ humiliated, crucified and glorified is the Way to the Father and the Truth; through faith in Him the believer has access to the Father.[. . .] Since the Father is the ultimate goal, He is greater than the Son.'[39] Although Käsemann objected to such language,[40] it is not unreasonable to describe the author's Christological understanding in terms of paradox, of majesty veiled in humility, because 'What the disciples should have apprehended on the mountain [of Transfiguration] — the ultimate context of God's glory in which Jesus must be set — is the apostolic presupposition upon which the gospel is based: the Word became flesh, and dwelt among us, and we beheld his glory (1:14); and this glory is not insisted upon by any emphasizing of the glorious achievements of the earthly ministry, but increases, rather, as the hour of suffering draws near, and is consummated in the supreme humiliation of the Passion.'[41]

Since Christology, which is ubiquitous in the Fourth Gospel, is not a doctrine on its own but is set within the framework of a gospel narrative, it serves to raise the wider question of the relation of history to what escapes purely historical description. This question is dominant throughout Hoskyns' commentary, and it is over his treatment of it that issue has been chiefly joined.

Two attempts are made in the introduction to deal with historical questions raised by the Fourth Gospel, 'The Historical Tension of the Fourth Gospel' and 'The Fourth Gospel and the Meaning of History'.[42] On any showing this is a perilous undertaking because the Fourth Gospel is not a historical work in the sense that it is possible to use it for a direct reconstruction of the words and deeds of Jesus; yet without the historical Jesus the work could never have been penned. It might be argued that the Gospel gives a theological picture of Jesus through the eyes of one who was a member of the emerging Church. Certainly the author thought of the Apostles primarily as those through whose words later generations of believers would come into being (17:20, 20:31), although his Gospel contains no mention of the institutional Church or of the Apostles as administrators of an organised community. If our knowledge of the historical Jesus and of the historical circumstances in which the Gospel was written are found to be as tantalisingly vague as they appear to be, what authority ought to be given to the Gospel as an authentic witness to Jesus and to the Church's understanding of him in relation to themselves and to God?

Some scholars have seen Hoskyns' dictum that it is the 'non-historical that makes sense of history' as serving to evade major historical questions posed by the Gospel, in its relation both to the historical Jesus and to the environment in which it was composed. This is especially so because Hoskyns' introduction did not deal with the 'normal' questions posed in introductions to biblical books, such as date, authorship or the circumstances which led to the book's composition. Thus A.M. Ramsey commented: 'Allowing that history means fact plus meaning, it is none the less inevitable to ask, more pressingly than Hoskyns ever asked, what happened and what does the evangelist himself believe to have happened.'[43] This may be set alongside the comment of C.H. Dodd: 'Its author and its editor [Hoskyns and Davey] deprecate the preoccupation of critics with the problem of "historicity"; they regard with suspicion any attempt to distinguish between the facts themselves and their interpretation; and discourage any expectation of finding an answer to the question whether the Fourth Evangelist had command of trustworthy information upon the facts beyond that which is accessible to us in the Synoptic Gospels. Yet they recognize, and state with all possible emphasis, that the Johannine theology has its centre in the historical person and the historical action of Jesus Christ. "The historical tension of the Fourth Gospel" (they say) is not to be lightly resolved by any theory which would lay the evangelist under "the charge of inventing history, or of using it merely as symbolism". But if this is so, it appears to bring us back by a different approach to the problem of historicity.'[44] This defect Dodd had already noted in Hoskyns' commentary when he reviewed it: 'I do not see how we can be prevented from raising the question (answering it is a different matter). What value is to be assigned to the record of the facts of which sense is to be made?'[45] Thus a choice has been laid before students of the Fourth Gospel. Either they wrestle with Hoskyns' standpoint that 'it is therefore extremely difficult to gain from the gospel any direct information concerning its original readers, and for this reason it is hard to come by the key to its historical understanding'[46] and hence concentrate on the author's historical perspectives from the point of view of theology; or they attempt to put historical meat on to the author's historical bones.

Since Hoskyns there have been notable attempts to reconstruct for the Fourth Gospel a genuine historical tradition, possibly independent of the synoptic tradition, which can be taken as a reliable source of historical fact. Perhaps the most notable of these attempts is that of C.H. Dodd. After a careful survey of the evidence, he is led to the conclusion that 'behind the Fourth Gospel lies an ancient tradition independent of the other gospels, and meriting serious consideration as a contribution to our knowledge of the historical facts concerning Jesus Christ.'[47] This tradition is assumed to be oral, but the possibility is not ruled out that some parts of it may have been written by way of aide-memoire, in which case written sources may have stood between the earlier oral tradition and the Fourth Gospel. The tradition found its origin in a Jewish milieu because, in the Evangelist's use of it, 'Aramaic idioms are to be detected everywhere'; in passages which are closely parallel to the Synoptics he introduces Aramaic terms absent in the synoptic tradition, and he was himself 'probably a speaker of Aramaic'.[48] Allusion to well-attested Jewish beliefs are made, in particular to the belief that the Messiah would remain unknown until Elijah identified him. Contact is also made with points of Jewish tradition, such as that relating to the adherence of five disciples — Andrew, Peter, Philip, Nathaniel and one who remains anonymous. Here Dodd notes the parallel rabbinic tradition — which he believes can hardly be accidental — that Jesus had five disciples, Mattai, Naqai, Netser, Buni and Toda.[49] Dodd makes much of the geographical, topographical and chronological setting of this tradition within southern Palestine. The Evangelist, he maintains, supplies Greek equivalents to Hebrew or Aramaic place-names as a concession to Greek readers,[50] and he is said to be well informed about the topography of Jerusalem and the south, whereas he is less so about Galilee and the north. While appearing ignorant concerning some northern place-names found in the Synoptics — e.g. Gennesaret, Chorazin and Caesarea Philippi —, he knows of southern place-names — Aenon, Salim, Bethany beyond Jordan — which are absent from the synoptic tradition. Thus this basic tradition on which the Evangelist worked was shaped 'in a Jewish-Christian environment still in touch with the synagogue, in Palestine, at a relatively early date, at any rate before the rebellion of A.D. 66'.[51]

In the last few decades this approach has proved popular, at least among scholars in Britain. J.A.T. Robinson, A.M. Hunter and S.S. Smalley have also argued that the Fourth Evangelist intended to supply historically verifiable information regarding the life and teaching of Jesus, and furthermore that historical traditions of great worth can be disentangled from interpretative comments. This has also involved the hypothesis that John used an early Jewish source from southern Palestine and worked independently of the synoptic tradition. J.A.T. Robinson[52] set out to counter five generally accepted propositions about the Fourth Gospel: (1) that the Evangelist is dependent on sources; (2) that his background is other than that of the events and teaching he is purporting to record; (3) that he is not to be regarded seriously as a witness to the

Jesus of history, but simply to the Christ of faith; (4) that he represents the end-term of theological development in first-century Christianity; and (5) that he is not himself the Apostle John or a direct eye-witness. He argued that the background to the gospel is 'Palestine'. The Qumran material gives additional credence to this view, because 'for the first time they [the Qumran documents] present us with a body of thought which in date and place [southern Palestine in the first century B.C.-A.D.], as well as in fundamental, and not merely verbal, theological affinity, may really represent an actual background, not merely a possible environment, for the distinctive categories of the Gospel.'[53] The Evangelist is also said to be 'vindicated in his knowledge of the topography and institutions of Palestine prior to the Jewish war'.[54] This is a view shared by A.M. Hunter: 'Thus archaeological discovery has, at point after point, tended to confirm John's topography, even if all problems have not been finally solved.'[55] S.S. Smalley uses this line of argument in relation to Gabbatha: 'But in any case John's unique reference to this site is evidently historical, and even if we still cannot be sure where Gabbatha was to be found, we can be fairly certain that the fourth evangelist was in touch with early tradition when he referred to it.'[56] (Barrett, in reviewing Smalley, finds it hard to see the logic of this remark, especially in view of P. Benoit's refutation of L.H. Vincent's earlier identification of Gabbatha.[58])

Distinctive in this matter is J.L. Martyn, who takes a middle position and argues for a 'two-level' approach which to some extent accommodates Hoskyns' point of view. One level relates to what happened on a particular occasion in the past in the life of Jesus, while the other relates to the Evangelist's own time and environment. The story recorded in chapter 9 of the man born blind serves as an example. One aspect of the story is said to relate back to the argument which Jesus had with the religious leaders of his own time and to his healing miracles, but on another level it concerns the exclusion of Jewish Christians from the synagogue by the *birkath ha'minim* of *c*.85 A.D. Martyn puts the matter thus: 'Sometimes John presented the two levels by using a single word for a corresponding pair of actors *(hupēretai; archontes)*. Sometimes he did so by an unhistorical juxtaposing of two terms *(hoi archiereis kai hoi pharisaioi)*. John was not in either case playing a kind of code-game, nor was he trying to instruct members of his Church about points of correspondence between the Jewish hierarchy of Jesus' day and that of their own day. One may be confident that he did not intend his readers to analyse the *dramatis personae* in the way in which we have done it.

Indeed, I doubt that he was himself analytically conscious of what I have termed the two-level drama, for his major concern in this regard was to bear witness to the essential integrity of the *"einmalig"* [once only] drama of Jesus' earthly life and the contemporary drama in which the Risen Lord acts through his servants.'[59] It may be questioned whether this approach is not over-subtle and whether it can apply to the whole of the Gospel. It may be that it can be applied to chapter 9, but would it apply equally to, for example, the Farewell Discourses?

It could be argued that, in some measure, these approaches to Johannine history are blind alleys, their main weakness appearing in a comment of Smalley: '. . . . some parts of John's narrative are to be interpreted on a historical level, and others on a theological level.'[60] This does less than justice to the profundity of the Evangelist. Not only is there no untheological tradition about Jesus in any of the Gospels, but, as Hoskyns rightly observed, the purpose of the Fourth Evangelist was theological rather than chronological, and as a result theology and history can no longer be disentangled. Naturally the author asserted the primacy of history. It was vital for him that there was a Jesus of Nazareth who lived and died in Palestine, even though to give a chronologically accurate outline of his career was not part of the author's purpose. Rather, he sought to draw out by use of 'the gospel format', which had become established in the Church, the truly theological meaning of the life and death of the one whom he believed to be the Son of God, the man from above. It is this interpretation of the focus of all history, the Father's revelation in Jesus Christ, not historically accurate details, that is to be found in the Fourth Gospel. C.K. Barrett sums up the matter well: 'The whole truth (*hapanta*) about the invisible and unknown God is declared in the historical figure to which John points in his not literally historical narrative. The figure of Jesus does not (so John in effect declares) make sense when viewed as a national leader, a rabbi, or a *theois anēr*; he makes sense when in hearing him you hear the Father, when in looking at him you see the Father, and worship him.'[61]

This approach, which follows but enlarges that of Hoskyns, liberates from the necessity of finding the precise circumstances in which the Fourth Gospel was composed and particular literal bits of history about Jesus in what it relates. Furthermore, neither the circumstances nor the literal bits of history can be uncovered with any confidence. Frequently the Fourth Gospel has become victim to the dogmatic labels — Palestinian Judaism, diaspora Judaism via Philo, Hellenistic Judaism, Qumran Judaism, Hellenism or Gnosticism — which scholars have attached to it. Hoskyns' comment about 'the steady refusal of the Fourth Gospel to come to rest in any solution which conservative or radical scholars have propounded'[62] may be criticised for being vague, but it rescues the Gospel 'from particular settings to give it universal applicability',[63] revealing the restlessness and comprehensiveness of the author's mind.

One aspect of the Fourth Evangelist's understanding of history is his relation to whatever sources he may have used, in particular to the synoptic tradition, and especially to Mark. This is a very vexed question. The most radical view of John's sources has been that of Bultmann, who believed that the *Offenbarungsreden* (roughly equivalent to what scholars generally call 'the discourses') were Gnostic documents which John 'Christianised' and 'historicised' by combining them with *Sēmeia Quelle* ('Signs source') in his account of Jesus. According to Bultmann, the *Sēmeia Quelle* contained a collection of miracle stories, comprising the changing of water into wine at Cana, the nobleman's son, the feeding, the walking on the water, the lame man, the blind man and the raising of Lazarus, to which were added the call of the disciples, which formed an introduction, and a shorter version of the story of the Samaritan woman. This source can be detected from the numbering of the first two miracles in it (2:11; 4:54), and from the summary statements in 12:37–39 and 20:30–1 which form its conclusion, but also from its stylistic traits.[64] The stories are said to be akin to those of the synoptic tradition, but have been revised by the Evangelist because they were originally marked by a somewhat superstitious belief in the miraculous, and represented Jesus as a *theios anēr*, whereas the Evangelist himself understood the signs as a symbolic representation of Jesus' revelation which challenged men to an existential decision about themselves. The *Offenbarungsreden*, according to Bultmann, can be isolated by their rhythmical quality as having been written in verse, whereas the Evangelist wrote in prose. The 'I' of the speaker in this source was not Jesus but the mythological figure of the Gnostic Revealer. Thus these discourses, which were non-Christian in origin, were adapted by the disciples of John the Baptist. When the Evangelist, who was originally a member of 'the Baptist sect', became a Christian he took over these Gnostic discourses and re-shaped them as utterances of Jesus. As a result, much of what has been known as the distinctively 'Johannine presentation' of Jesus — the Prologue, the 'I am' sayings, and the majority of the discourse material — existed in a source which was not Christian at all but Gnostic both in origin and content.

Two major questions emerge from such an analysis. Is it possible to detect sources in this way in the gospel, and what are the implications for our understanding of the gospel if, at least in the case of one source, the original context is said to be non-Christian? The difficulty with the first question is simply that of detection. As no parallel documents are involved, the procedure can only be carried on by an internal literary criticism of the gospel itself. In spite of the detail of Bultmann's literary analyses, the impression remains that his source criticism is based on a degree of enlightened guesswork and a measure of prejudice about the effectiveness of the exercise. It is not clear that there are enough passages identifiable as coming from the Evangelist's own hand when they are compared with the rest of the material to give a clear indication of his style. There is the added difficulty, as Barrett has observed with reference to the Prologue,[65] of separating 'verse' from 'prose'. The question is, given the constraints of knowledge and the vulnerability of the exercise, whether Bultmann's source hypothesis is either possible or provable. The seriousness of the hypothesis lies in Bultmann's belief that he had discovered the key to the author's method and theology precisely from the detection of how a non-Christian source is Christianised, and thus raising the question not only of whether this is the 'right' key to the understanding of the gospel, but whether it is, as for Bultmann, the only key. In the end, the student of the Fourth Gospel has to decide which view is more likely to have been correct: the Bultmann view that the author's development as a theologian was dictated by external influences such as the Gnostic Redeemer myth, or the Hoskyns view that the profundity of the Evangelist's mind developed by meditating upon the synoptic tradition and enlarging upon it.

For Hoskyns 'any attempt to expose the background of the Fourth Gospel must therefore begin with a comparison between it and the synoptic gospels, and must be conducted in the hope that this comparison will reveal some strict relationship, if not between the Fourth Gospel and the synoptic gospels, at least between it and the tradition that has been preserved in them.'[66] This beginning is necessary because the Fourth Gospel will be proved true or false by it, the vital test being whether or not 'the Marcan narrative becomes more intelligible after reading the Fourth Gospel.'[67] Here Hoskyns' views about the character and authority of the work return into play, as he believed that 'the Church clearly intends the book to be read in close connection with the earlier gospels, and not as an isolated independent work.'[68] He then proceeded to examine how episodes recorded in the synoptic gospels are woven into one consistent picture by the Fourth Evangelist, and how he has used, omitted and modified earlier tradition, with the caveat that 'the Fourth Gospel is wholly misunderstood when it is regarded as a haven of rest at which the Church arrived after the turmoil of the synoptic gospels. . . .'[69]

This 'strict relationship' between the Fourth Gospel and the earlier synoptic Gospels was, however, challenged by Percy Gardner-Smith, who asked the question whether or not 'it is easier to account for the similarities between St John and the Synoptists without a theory of literary dependence, or to explain the discrepancies if such a theory has been accepted.'[70] Gardner-Smith then proceeded to analyse stories in the Fourth Gospel which are found in the synoptics, enquiring how the resemblances and differences are best explained. He concluded that the resemblances are best explained on the basis of oral tradition, and that there is no substance to the view that the author knew any of the synoptic Gospels as written works because even 'the outline of any written Gospel was determined not only by the natural sequence of history, but also by the form of the preaching of the apostles and their immediate followers.'[71] This, he admitted, had implications in related areas.[72] Thus it could be that the Fourth Gospel should be dated earlier than the end of the first century and that it contains material of 'historical trustworthiness' apart from the synoptics. Once the 'synoptics-Fourth Gospel strict relationship' had been broken, it meant that, in scholarly debate at least, other issues were brought into the arena, with the result that the various problems — of dating, of the synoptic link, of the historical trustworthiness of all (or some) of the author's sources and of the very question of sources itself — have become interwoven.

In this question Gardner-Smith has been followed by others, including C.H. Dodd, who commented: 'Definite evidence pointing to documentary relations between John and the Synoptics is seen to be singularly sparse when once the presumption in favour of such relations is abandoned.'[73] This trend has been continued in more recent commentaries. R.E. Brown, while noting with favour a growing consensus towards this position, modifies it to the extent that he recognises that within what he believes to be the five-stage redaction of the Gospel there may have been minor cross-influences from the Synoptic tradition.[74] Similarly, Barnabas Lindars observes that 'most scholars today favour the view that John made use of independent parallel traditions . . . the difficulty [of accounting for the verbal parallels between the Fourth Gospel and the Synoptics] is overcome if we assume that John's sources were at some points either identical with, or closely similar to, the sources used by Mark and Luke. There is no reason why some at least of these sources should not have been in written form.'[75]

This, however, may beg as many questions as it answers. Thus, is it any longer possible to discern these independent parallel traditions? And how are sources either identical with, or closely similar to, sources used by Mark and Luke to be detected? It may be that the case argued by Hoskyns ought to be re-opened, for he had at least the advantage of arguing from the known (the Fourth Gospel) back to another known (the Gospel of Mark). He was aware of the subtlety of the position 'if not between the Fourth Gospel and the synoptic gospels, at least between it and the tradition that has been preserved in them', but he did not fall into the trap (as does Lindars?) of attempting to distinguish between Mark and the oral tradition on which it was based or the written source from which it drew. As Barrett has commented, 'All that can be said is that we do not have before us the oral tradition on which Mark was based; we do not have any of the written source that Mark may have quoted; but we do have Mark, and in Mark are the stories that John repeats, sometimes at least with similar or even identical words, sometimes at least in substantially the same order . . . the fact is that there crops up repeatedly in John evidence that suggests that the evangelist knew a body of traditional material that either was Mark, or was something much like Mark; and anyone who after an interval of nineteen centuries feels himself in a position to distinguish nicely between "Mark" and "something much like Mark" is at liberty to do so.'[76]

What is possibly more important is Hoskyns' question whether the Marcan narrative becomes more intelligible after reading the Fourth Gospel.[77] Another way of asking the question is to enquire how the Fourth Evangelist 'used' Mark and perhaps other elements in the Synoptic tradition. Having largely broken the link between the Fourth Gospel and the Synoptics, scholars have paid little attention to the Johannine use of the Marcan/synoptic tradition. The word 'use' must be carefully analysed when applied to Gospel study. It is generally agreed that Matthew used Mark. This means that Matthew took over large sections of the Marcan narrative, which he placed within the fivefold structure of his Gospel as a framework for the sayings of Jesus. In his Passion narrative Matthew's method is obvious: 'he takes over the Marcan narrative, adding 'legendary' details of his own, such as the dream of Pilate's wife (Matt. 27:19). Whatever may be said about 'Q', it is certain that Matthew 'used' 'Q' in a way different from that in which he 'used' Mark. 'Q' is used more spasmodically and is more interwoven with his own source, 'M'. But how did the Fourth Evangelist 'use' Mark? Clearly in a way different from the way Matthew 'used' either Mark or 'Q'. It may be suggested that the Fourth Evangelist took the synoptic tradition and probed its inner meaning. He did not import it as foreign matter into the Gospel; Bultmann suggested that a later editor had added redactional information from the synoptic tradition in order to make the Gospel more acceptable to orthodox opinion.[78] Rather the author sought to give fresh meaning to what he believed to be inadequately expressed in the earlier tradition. This can be seen in chapter 6, where the author used the miracles of Jesus feeding the multitude and walking on the lake, which had already been combined in the Marcan tradition,[79] and built upon them to illustrate what feeding upon the flesh and blood of the Son of man meant.[80]

But what of the synoptic material which the Fourth Evangelist omitted? In the Fourth Gospel, both the baptism and the transfiguration are ignored, together with the agony of Jesus in Gethsemane, of which only traces remain in 12:27–30 and 18:11. This, however, could have been deliberate on the part of the author and not because he was unaware of these events. Instead he wished to show that the heavenly glory of Jesus, as revealed in the transfiguration and in the fact that he enters completely into humanity because he is completely human, condition every part of his life. When his readers read in the prologue 'We have beheld his glory' (1:14), their minds would have been directed to consider the incarnate life of Jesus, where his triumph and humiliation were constant themes, as was his obedience to the Father's will. It was this Evangelist's task to remain faithful to the themes expressed in the Synoptic Gospels while at one and the same time modifying, co-ordinating and clarifying them in order to demonstrate more powerfully their inner meaning.

C.K. Barrett, in his revision of an earlier work of W.F. Howard which sketched the criticism and interpretation of the Fourth Gospel from 1901 to 1931, expressed the belief that the three authors with whom he is concerned in his analysis of interpretation from 1931 to 1953 — Hoskyns, Bultmann and Dodd — all deal with John, to a greater extent than previously, as a theological writer, although they come to different conclusions. 'Recent exposition as a whole has been marked by the recognition that John is a work of theology — and, further, of biblical theology. The commentator's work is seen to remain incomplete when he has laid bare the sources of the Gospel, rearranged it in its supposed original order,[81] and on this basis estimated its historical value. Nor has he fulfilled a theological task when he has drawn out a series of parallels between John and other religious literature of the same period. John, no less than Mark or Romans, is a setting-forth of the Christian proclamation of the mighty acts of judgement and mercy wrought by God in Jesus Christ for the redemption of the world. The eternal counsels of God, his acts in history, and the consequences of these acts, are described, and described in relation to the biblical revelation as a whole — that is, in particular, to the Old Testament.'[82] Thus Hoskyns interprets Johannine theology by beginning with the biblical world and Christian tradition, and never really moving outside it; Dodd does so by seeing the Gospel as an attempt to communicate the Christian message to the Hellenistic world, and Bultmann does so by attempting to detect how material of non-Christian origin was Christianised and incorporated into the Gospel and hence adapted by the Evangelist to its new, biblical, environment.

Although Dodd and Bultmann refer to individual parts of Hoskyns' exegesis of John with approval, it is with his general presuppositions that they, in their differing ways, have difficulty. For Hoskyns the Fourth Gospel is both a 'Catholic' and a 'restless' book. However, Bultmann and Käsemann have difficulty with 'Catholicity' and with Hoskyns' interpretation of it. For them the Fourth Gospel is to be set within 'sectarian' Christianity on the fringe of the Church, and in Bultmann's view non-Christian material — not very far removed from the Christian position of the church to which the Gospel is addressed — has been used in composition. They have a different view from Hoskyns of the relationship between the development of the Gospel and the origins of the Christian religion and of the extent to which the Evangelist has departed from 'biblical tradition', which for Hoskyns is 'apostolic Christianity'.

For Hoskyns, especially after his acquaintance with Schlatter's commentary, set the Gospel in what many commentators have declared to be too narrow confines. Even C.K. Barrett, an admirer of Hoskyns' work who accepts many of his conclusions (or what might have been his conclusions),[83] maintains the lack of a radical analysis of 'other spirits' to be its principal weakness.[84] However, the investigation of 'other spirits' on the fringe of Judaism, and outside it, who have made their contribution to the creation of a distinctively Johannine theology, need not necessarily lead to the conclusions of Bultmann and Käsemann.

Hoskyns saw the Fourth Gospel equally as a 'restless' book. Dodd, anxious to give the material more definite anchoring, set it within the Church's missionary endeavour; this also led him, and others such as Robinson and Smalley who follow his particular approach to the Gospel, to argue for its 'historical trustworthiness'. In doing so they call into question Hoskyns' solution to the problem — of the relation of history to what is above or beyond history — which John, because of his narrative form, raises. Thus it was possible for Robert Kysar to speak of a consensus of scholarly opinion regarding the Gospel: 'First John did not use the synoptic gospels, even though he may have drawn some of the material from a tradition having some points of contact with the synoptic oral tradition; second, some interest in the genre of Johannine *Reden* seemed to be arising; and third, the fundamentally Semitic background of the Johannine tradition seemed agreed upon, thanks in part to the discoveries at Qumran.'[85] Such a consensus may explain why Hoskyns' commentary, which calls in question some of the points on which this consensus is based, has been underestimated. It may be that John as 'an editor' of the synoptic tradition has been too easily abandoned, and that this tradition, especially Mark, remains the only detectable 'source' for the Gospel. Perhaps, most important of all, Hoskyns' presentation of John as a theologian who interprets history theologically needs to be given more attention by modern scholarship.

Hoskyns was above all anxious that the Fourth Gospel should speak in its own way and on its own terms, the purpose of his commentary being to illuminate rather than to impose. 'In introducing the reader to the study of the Fourth Gospel it seemed supremely necessary to demand that he should take it seriously. It has not seemed so necessary to overwhelm him with information that will free him from the onus of reading what the Evangelist actually wrote, that will enable him to talk about the Gospel or sit for an examination upon it without having read it or sought to digest it.'[86]

NOTES

1. R. Bultmann, *The Gospel of John*, Eng. transl. Oxford, 1971. In his revision of the original German edition, it is clear that Bultmann has used Hoskyns' commentary. Evidence is provided by p. 14, note 1, where he quotes Hoskyns' view that 'the Prologue . . . is not so much a preface to the Gospel as a summary of it', and p. 673, note 5, where 'according to Hoskyns Jesus inclines his head to his Mother and to the Disciple and

"handed over the Spirit", namely to the believers who stand under the cross.'

2. ibid., p. 367. Here Bultmann complains that C.K. Barrett 'does not take sufficient notice of the decisive differences'. Note 3.

3. ibid.

4. *The Fourth Gospel*, p. 132.

5. ibid., p. 50.

6. Bultmann, *John*, p. 165, note 1. Note also *The Fourth Gospel*, p. 231, where Hoskyns, commenting on the same verses as Bultmann (3:31ff), writes: 'To have apprehended this relation between the audible words of Jesus and the inaudible words of God is to seal and authenticate and attest the truth of God . . . Herein is the love of God (cf. 3: 16, 5:20, 10:17; Mark 1:11. 9:7, 12:6) and the authority of Jesus (13:3, 17:2, 7, 22, 24).'

7. *The Fourth Gospel*, p. 81.

8. C.H. Dodd, *The Interpretation of the Fourth Gospel*, Cambridge, 1953.

9. The Hermetic literature represents a collection of Greek and Latin religious and philosophical writings ascribed to Hermes Trismegistus, a later designation of the Egyptian God, Thoth, who was believed to be the father and protector of all knowledge. The literature dates probably from between the middle of the first and the end of the third century A.D..

10. C.H. Dodd, review of The Fourth Gospel in *Theology*, XLI, 1940, p. 307; see also *Gore to Temple*: 'It has been a serious criticism of Hoskyns that he virtually ignored the Hellenistic background of the Fourth Gospel' (p. 140). F.W. Dillistone (*C.H. Dodd*, London, 1977, p. 165) believes that Dodd's *The Interpretation of the Fourth Gospel* was designed to repair the defect which he believed Hoskyns had made in the virtual ignoring of the Hellenistic background in his commentary.

11. C.H. Dodd, *The Interpretation of the Fourth Gospel*, Cambridge, 1953, p. 53.

12. ibid., p. 73.

13. ibid., p. 9.

14. Confirmed in a private letter from Dr F.W. Dillistone: 'The Review represents so fully Hoskyns' ideas that it might almost have been Hoskyns speaking.'

15. F.N. Davey, review of Dodd's *The Interpretation of the Fourth Gospel*, in *J.T.S.*, new series, IV, 1953, pp. 242f.

16. ibid., pp. 243f.

17. ibid., p. 244.

18. See *The Fourth Gospel*, p. 50: 'It is therefore extremely difficult to gain from the gospel any direct information concerning its original readers, and for this reason it is hard to come by the key to its historical understanding.' Also p. 129: 'For the Gospel refused to come to rest in any haven provided by historical or psychological (mystical) analysis.'

19. *The Fourth Gospel*, p. 90.

20. ibid., p. 92.
21. ibid., p. 131.
22. F.G. Downing, *The Church and Jesus: A Study in History, Philosophy and Theology*, S.B.T., 2nd series, 10, London, 1968. Note, for example, Downing's comment on p. 25: 'It is really difficult to "find" the early Church, to draw up an agreed account of its life and beliefs and practices.'
23. E. Käsemann, *The Testament of Jesus*, Eng. transl. London, 1968, p. 39.
24. ibid.
25. ibid., p. 40.
26. *The Fourth Gospel*, p. 97.
27. See, for example, Ignatius, Ep. to Smyrnaeans, 8, V, 2. 'Wheresoever the bishop appears, there let the people be, even as wheresoever Christ Jesus is, there is the Catholic Church.'
28. C.K. Barrett, *The Gospel according to St. John*, 2nd edn, London, 1978, pp. 142f.
29. *The Testament of Jesus*, pp. 27f.
30. John 20:21b, where Hoskyns comments: '. . . These are the men who must take up the work of the incarnate Son of God, and proclaim to the world the Gospel of salvation.[. . .] Since the conquest of the power of the world by the death and resurrection of Christ made the Christian mission to the world possible, the exposition of the wounds is at once followed first by the Apostolic commission of the disciples, secondly by their consecration (17:18, 19). They are made Apostles, the Apostles of the Son of God; as the Father has sent the Son, so the Son sends His disciples . . .' (*The Fourth Gospel*, p. 544).
31. ibid., pp. 129f.
32. ibid., p. 126. In the 1st edn of *The Fourth Gospel* (1940), 2 vols, this material formed an introductory essay, pp. xxi–xlviii, whereas in the 1-vol. 2nd edn (1947) this forms ch. 7, 'The Fourth Gospel and the Problem of the Meaning of History'. However, this is not mentioned by Davey in his note at the beginning of the 2nd edn dated 6 May 1947.
33. C.K. Barrett, 'Christocentric or Theocentric?', Observations on the Theological Method of the Fourth Gospel', in J. Coppens (ed.), *La Notion Biblique de Dieu*, Duculot, Louvain, 1976, p. 363.
34. *The Testament of Jesus*, p. 3, note 3.
35. ibid., p. 26.
36. *The Fourth Gospel*, p. 449. See also A.M. Ramsey, *The Glory of God and the Transfiguration of Christ*, p. 65.
37. 'Christocentric or Theocentric', p. 371.
38. ibid., p. 371.
39. *The Fourth Gospel*, p. 464. Hoskyns is here commenting on 14:28.
40. *The Testament of Jesus*, p. 11: 'The road travelled by the Johannine Christ should consequently not be presented as a development from lowliness to glory. But may we then speak instead of the paradox of a glory hidden in

lowliness?' For an alternative view, see S.S. Smalley, 'The Testament of Jesus: Another Look', *S.E.*, VI, 1973, pp. 495–501.

41. *The Fourth Gospel*, pp. 81f.
42. This latter article was largely composed by Davey, revealing his somewhat rhetorical style and tendency to obscurity.
43. *Gore to Temple*, p. 140.
44. Dodd, *Historical Tradition*, p. 4.
45. Theology, XLI, p. 309.
46. *The Fourth Gospel*, p. 50.
47. Dodd, *Historical Tradition*, p. 423.
48. ibid., p. 424.
49. ibid., pp. 303f, 425.
50. For example: Gabbatha, *lithostrōton* (John 19:13) and Golgotha, *kraniou topos* (John 19:17).
51. Dodd, *Historical Tradition*, p. 426.
52. J.A.T. Robinson, 'The New Look on the Fourth Gospel', in *Twelve New Testament Studies*, London, 1962, pp. 94–106. This was originally given as a lecture at an Oxford conference in 1957.
53. ibid., p. 99.
54. ibid., p. 101.
55. A.M. Hunter, *According to John*, London, 1968, p. 52.
56. S.S. Smalley, *John — Evangelist and Interpreter*, Exeter, 1978, p. 36.
57. *J.T.S.*, new series, XXX, 1979, pp. 536f.
58. P. Benoit, 'L'Antonia d'Hérode le Grand et le Forum Oriental d'Aelia Capitolina', *H.T.R.*, 64, 1971, pp. 135–67. Note also C.K. Barrett's comments, *St. John*, 2nd edn, p. 545: '. . . even if it were known that the site was called Gabbatha this could not prove the historicity of John's narrative . . . The buildings and paving in question belong to the second century and have nothing to do with the events of the Gospel.'
59. J.L. Martyn, *History and Theology in the Fourth Gospel*, New York, 1968, p. 77.
60. Smalley, op. cit., p. 178. See also C.K. Barrett's review of Smalley's book, *J.T.S.*, new series, XXX, 1979, p. 536f.
61. 'Christocentric or Theocentric?' p. 376.
62. *The Fourth Gospel*, p. 131.
63. C.K. Barrett, 'History', *Essays on John*, London, 1982, p. 139. 'Restless' is Hoskyns' term, *The Fourth Gospel*, p. 19, while 'comprehensive' is that of Barrett, 'History', op. cit., pp. 125f and 130.
64. Bultmann does not give a complete list of the passages which make up these sources in his commentary. They are, however, usefully set out by D.M. Smith, *The Composition and Order of the Fourth Gospel: Bultmann's literary theory*, London, 1965: the *Sēmeia Quelle*, pp. 38–44, the *Offenbarungsreden*, pp. 23–34. On signs, see also R.T. Fortna, *The Gospel of Signs*, Cambridge, 1970.

65. C.K. Barrett, 'The Prologue of St. John's Gospel', *New Testament Essays*, London, 1972, p. 39.
66. *The Fourth Gospel*, pp. 59f.
67. ibid., p. 133.
68. ibid., p. 68.
69. ibid., p. 61.
70. P. Gardner-Smith, *St. John and the Synoptic Gospels*, Cambridge, 1938, p. x.
71. ibid., p. 88.
72. ibid., p. 93f.
73. C.H. Dodd, *The Interpretation of the Fourth Gospel*, op. cit., p. 449.
74. R.E. Brown, *The Gospel according to John I–XII*, New York, 1966.
75. B. Lindars, *The Gospel of John*, London, 1972, pp. 26f.
76. C.K. Barrett, *The Gospel according to St. John*, 2nd edn, London, 1978, p. 45. Until quite recently, with the exception of Barrett, almost all Johannine specialists denied any link between John and the Synoptics. However F. Neirynck ('John and the Synoptics: The Empty Tomb Stories', *N.T.S.*, 30, 1984, p. 161) believes that the matter is being opened up again, and quotes D.M. Smith, 'John and the Synoptics: Some Dimensions of the Problem', *N.T.S.*, 26, 1980, pp. 425–44, as confirmation of this. Smith concludes: 'I am beginning to be able to conceive of a scenario in which John knew, or knew of, the synoptics.[. . .] Possibly the Fourth Gospel can be adequately explained . . . without denying the fourth evangelist's awareness of them [the synoptic gospels]' (pp. 443f.).
77. Hoskyns used in a more interesting way the dictum of B.H. Streeter that 'clearly the facts so far stated amount to little short of a demonstration that John knew the Gospel of Mark and knew it well' (*The Four Gospels*, London, 1924, p. 400).
78. R. Bultmann, *John*, for example, pp. 234f on 6:51b–59, where he believes that 'the editor . . . has added or inserted a secondary interpretation of the bread of life in terms of the Lord's Supper.'
79. The passages in question are Mark 6: 34–44 — John 6: 1–13; Mark 6: 45–52 — John 6: 16–21.
80. For more details see C.K. Barrett, 'The Flesh of the Son of Man, John 6:53', in *Essays on John*, London, 1982, pp. 37–49.
81. W.F. Howard, *The Fourth Gospel in Recent Criticism and Interpretation*, rev. edn by C.K. Barrett, London, 1955, sets out the various theories of Partition and Redaction of the Gospel in Appendix C, pp. 297–302. Bultmann has the most radical re-ordering of text so that only 1:1–4:54 (except for minor alterations in ch. 3) and 18:1–20:31 are left intact. Bultmann's re-ordered text has been outlined by D.M. Smith, op. cit., pp. 178–212. Hoskyns was clear that 'the Fourth Gospel is, as it stands, a literary unity' (*The Fourth Gospel*, pp. 68f). It might also be argued that it makes the best theological sense as it now stands.

82. W.F. Howard, op. cit., p. 243. This particular chapter was written by Barrett.

83. C.K. Barrett, *The Gospel according to St. John*, 2nd edn, London, 1978, preface, p. viii: 'To some of the most popular modern opinions I do not subscribe. I do not believe that Qumran holds the key to John; I do not believe that it is a Palestinian work, aimed at Diaspora Judaism; I do not believe that it is possible to isolate sources, unless perhaps we should describe Mark as a source; I do not believe that John intended to supply us with historically verifiable information regarding the life and teaching of Jesus, and that historical traditions of great worth can be disentangled from his interpretative comments. I believe that John does more to interpret the Nag Hammadi texts than they do to interpret John.'

84. C.K. Barrett, *The Gospel of John and Judaism*, London, 1975, pp. 5f.

85. R. Kysar, 'The Source Analysis of the Fourth Gospel — a growing consensus?', *Nov. T.*, 15, 1973, p. 134.

86. *The Fourth Gospel*, pp. 134f.

CONCLUSION

In his introductory comments, as he began his editorship of *the Journal of New Testament Studies*, G.N. Stanton advanced the view that New Testament scholars might now be taking more interest in the theological and hermeneutical concerns in their work than they did thirty years ago when the journal was first published. According to Stanton evidence for this is provided by the fact that the last two presidents of the Society for New Testament Studies, B. Reicke and R.H. Fuller, have discussed the contributions to biblical theology of 'two giants of the past', W.M.L. de Wette and E.C. Hoskyns.[1] Fuller maintains that Hoskyns and his biblical theology 'were not merely a detour'[2] but of lasting value to biblical scholarship. But how is this so and what aspects of Hoskyns' work have continuing relevance?

This process of evaluation was brought full circle by the publication in 1981 of the posthumous work *Crucifixion-Resurrection*, which was not fully completed by the time of Hoskyns' death in June 1937. The problem is that this work is not what it seems. It is not a carefully argued systematic analysis of the portrayal by the New Testament writers of the crucifixion and resurrection of Christ but rather a number of shafts sunk into the subject. The result is that despite some brilliant flashes of insight, the finished product is somewhat ill-organised and incomplete. This makes the question of what here will be of lasting value to biblical scholarship difficult to determine. This in turn raises the question of the progress of Hoskyns' thought after the publication of *The Riddle of the New Testament* in 1931 and his translation of Barth's *The Epistle to the Romans* in 1933. In no way can *Crucifixion-Resurrection* be said to be a sequel to *The Riddle of the New Testament* in the sense that it developed theologically the historical and critical thesis already outlined in *The Riddle*. In this is to be found a carefully ordered argument for the general reader, whereas in *Crucifixion-Resurrection* the style is more diffuse and the overall trend more difficult to follow. The 'resurrection' part is hardly dealt with, and so the incomplete manuscript breaks off at the most inconvenient point possible.

A picture thus emerges towards the end of 1933 of Hoskyns' thought losing some of the clarity of earlier years and becoming more fragmentary and perhaps restless. This may have been partly due to the effort needed in the translation of Barth's *Romans*. Although the translation has been described as brilliant, it represented many months of hard labour and it is said that this cost him dear. After it Hoskyns' own style became more rhetorical and lacking in the directness that had characterised so much of his earlier work. This can be illustrated by a comparison between the revised and unrevised sections of his commentary on the Fourth Gospel, the revised section being rewritten after his translation of Barth's *Romans*.[3]

Before his death Hoskyns had revised his commentary up to 6:31. In this section it can be seen that the theological concentration is greater and the construction tighter, with a plentiful use of antithesis and paradox to emphasise the gap between the transcendent and the earthly, the historical and the non-historical and, supremely, between God and man. This has led to the judgement that the revised section is 'more an exercise in the philosophy of religion than a commentary on a biblical book'. Whether or not this exercise has in the end led to a greater understanding of the Fourth Gospel must be left to individual judgement. Perhaps it has to be admitted that the task is almost too difficult because it poses the almost unanswerable question of how a biblical book can 'speak' to future generations. It may be that in his attempt to do this the charge of 'rhetoric' can be used against Hoskyns, because in the end the text must speak for itself and any verbal dressing-over can only serve to obscure the author's intentions. The reader is left wondering whether he is really listening to the voice of the Fourth Evangelist or to the voice of Karl Barth as mirrored through Hoskyns.

It is therefore not unreasonable to advance the view that the unrevised section of the commentary may be of more lasting value to the student of the Fourth Gospel. In this the reader is taken with directness, clarity and insight through the theological approach of the Fourth Evangelist, examining how this theology springs from the witness of the apostolic Church and Christ and how it is related to the New Testament as a whole. There are valuable references to the use of John in patristic exegesis not found in other commentaries, and useful detached notes on such subjects as 'The Liturgical Use of the Pedilavium', provided as a help to the understanding of the foot-washing in chapter 13.

The revised section may suffer in another way, namely the anchoring of the Fourth Gospel more firmly within the context of Judaism. This was due to the influence on Hoskyns of the commentary by Adolf Schlatter. Because it had been published in 1930, reference to this commentary is totally absent from the unrevised part whereas in revision Hoskyns referred to it frequently. This had a narrowing effect and in some measure contradicted Hoskyns' earlier opinion that the author 'has done his best, apparently with intention, to cover up his tracks',[4] and that it was 'extremely difficult to gain from the gospel any direct information concerning its original readers, and for this reason it is hard to come by the key to its historical understanding.'[5] But through Schlatter Hoskyns has placed the Fourth Gospel firmly within the track of Judaism. It could be said that this both limits the commentary and affects its lasting value as a work of scholarship because it fails to take into account the Fourth Evangelist's use of a vast spectrum of material and his appeal to an audience wider than Judaism.

It could be argued, then, that Hoskyns' most fruitful period in relation to biblical theology is that from 1926 to the publication of *The Riddle of the New Testament* in 1931. Two major essays were published by him during this period, 'The Christ of the Synoptic Gospels' in *Essays Catholic and Critical* and 'Jesus the Messiah' in *Mysterium Christi*. These are classical attempts to deal with the questions of christology and the 'status' of the Gospel material within this. They are essays to which scholars ought to be continually referring because they are such important landmarks in the discussion. Hoskyns maintained that the contradictory elements found within the synoptic tradition find their synthesis and focus with Jesus himself. What is more, the characteristic features of the Catholic religion formulated in the early Christian centuries have their origin in Jesus' interpretation of his Person and of the significance of his disciples for the world. Conversely the Catholicism of succeeding generations must be tested by the religion which the New Testament as a whole provides.

It is of little value for scholars to complain that Hoskyns' work is 'dated' because he did not take into account the newly-developing discipline of form criticism in his evaluation of the synoptic material. True, form criticism was to uncover the possibility that multiple and varied influences had been at work upon individual parts of the synoptic tradition on its way from Jesus to the Gospel writers, but Hoskyns' work remains important source material of a preliminary kind and is a useful corrective to some of the form critics who made the material appear so multiple and varied that it lost any kind of overall cohesion and synthesis.

Hoskyns' association with the group which produced the *Mysterium Christi* volume highlights another aspect of his contribution to biblical studies, namely the links he forged with German scholars. Given that he received his theological training from Adolf Harnack in Berlin and lectured to the University of Tübingen when he was still a curate, he saw clearly the insularity of English theological work. Encouraged by George Bell, an Anglo-German group of scholars met to discuss major theological issues such as the Kingdom of God, Christology and the Church. Hoskyns hoped that some of his own students would spend time at a German university, and many did so. This meant that a later generation would not be as insular as their forefathers had been, and would ensure that German thinking became part of the English theological tradition. The fact that this happened, even years after Hoskyns' death, owes much to his pioneering zeal in this area.

Any scholar must be seen within the context of his own time and place. In Hoskyns' case time was 'inter-war' and place was the University of Cambridge, in particular Corpus Christi College. Somewhat surprisingly a great interest has developed in our own time in things 'inter-war', the period 1918–39 becoming an attractive field for both 'popular' and 'professional' audiences. An important aspect of this interest must be in the area of religion. Without doubt, although his biblical theology was fragmentary and incomplete, Hoskyns has made a major contribution to our understanding of the religion of this period. Part of this interest derives from the fact that he said things contrary to the general theological trend, especially in Cambridge. He emphasised the transcendence of God, the 'cost' of the Cross and the otherworldliness in religion which was at variance with what many of his colleagues were saying. With him theology, especially New Testament theology, became exciting and dynamic and, despite the limitations of its incompleteness, his work remains a firm basis on which others can build.

Behind Hoskyns the theologian was Hoskyns the teacher, priest and preacher. Here lecture-room, altar and pulpit are united. This synthesis is surely necessary in theology, which is not just the preserve of universities but also of the Church and indeed the world. The issues facing theology remain, and it may be that a patient study of Hoskyns' work provides some of the clues to the unresolved questions that remain.

NOTES

1. G.N. Stanton, 'The Passing of an Era?', *N.T.S.*, 30, p. 2.
2. R.H. Fuller, 'Sir Edwyn Hoskyns and the Contemporary Relevance of 'Biblical Theology', *N.T.S.*, 30, p. 344.
3. *The Fourth Gospel*, p. 8.
4. ibid., p. 18.
5. ibid., p. 50.

THE PUBLISHED WORKS OF
SIR EDWYN HOSKYNS

1920

'Genesis 1–11 and St. John's Gospel', *J.T.S.*, XXI, pp. 210–18.
'Adversaria Exegetica: St. John III: 1–21', *Theology*, I, pp. 83–9.
'Adversaria Exegetica: The Old and the New Worship of God: St. John II: 13–22', *Theology*, I, pp. 143–8.

1921

'Adversaria Exegetica: The Good Shepherd, St. John X: 1–18', *Theology*, II, pp. 202–7.
Reviews of H. Shears, *The Gospel according to Paul*; A.H. McNeile, *St. Paul*; A. Nairne, *The Faith of the New Testament*; A. Nairne, *The Epistle to the Hebrews*, *J.T.S.*, XXII, pp. 184–9.

1922

'Catholicism in Germany', *Theology*, V, pp. 257–62.
Review of F.J. Foakes-Jackson and K. Lake (eds), *The Beginnings of Christianity*, Part I, *Theology*, VI, pp. 298–304.

1923

Christ and Catholicism, Anglo-Catholic Congress Books, 12.
'Adversaria Exegetica: But after I am risen I will go before you into Galilee (Mark XIV: 28)', *Theology*, VII, pp. 147–55.

1925

Review of D.S. Guy, *Was Holy Communion instituted by Jesus?*, *J.T.S.*, XXVI, pp. 203f.

1926

'The Christ of the Synoptic Gospels' in E.G. Selwyn (ed.), *Essays Catholic and Critical*, London, pp. 151–78.

1927

('The Eternal Spirit': [b]) 'In the Epistles of St Paul and in the Writings of St John', *The Spirit in Life and Thought*, Papers read and Addresses delivered at the Southport Church Congress, London and Liverpool, pp. 88–97.
'The Eucharist in the New Testament', Anglo-Catholic Congress Report, pp. 51–6.

'The Other-Worldly Kingdom of God in the New Testament', contribution to the Canterbury Anglo-German Conference, *Theology*, XIV, pp. 249–55.

Review of R. Bultmann, *Jesus*, *J.T.S.*, XXVIII, pp. 106–9.

'Some New Testament Teachings about the Holy Spirit: I. The Holy Spirit in St. Luke's Gospel', *The Sign*, July.

'Some New Testament Teachings about the Holy Spirit: II. The Holy Spirit in the Epistle to the Ephesians', *The Sign*, August.

1928

'Jesus Christ Son of God Saviour', contribution to the Wartburg Anglo-German Conference, *Theology*, XVII, pp. 215–7.

'The Johannine Epistles' in C. Gore, H.L. Goudge and A. Guillaume (eds), *A New Commentary on Holy Scripture*, London, pp. 658–73.

Review of B.W. Bacon, *The Story of Jesus and the Beginnings of the Church*, *Theology*, XVII, pp. 173–5.

Review of T.L. Haitjema, *Karl Barth's Kritische Theologie*, *J.T.S.*, XXIX, pp. 201–4.

Review of A.H. McNeile, *An Introduction to the Study of the New Testament*, *C.Q.R.*, CV, pp. 367–70.

1929

Review of O.C. Quick, *The Christian Sacraments*; H.J. Wotherspoon, *Religious Values in the Sacraments*; C.R. Smith, *The Sacramental Society*, *J.T.S.*, XXX, pp. 86–9.

Review of A.L. Lilley, *Sacraments: A Study in Some Moments in the attempt to define their meaning for Christian Worship*; L. Hodgson, *And Was Made Man*; H.M. Foston, *The Evening of the Last Supper*, *J.T.S.*, XXX, pp. 418–24.

1930

'The Apostolicity of the Church', Anglo-Catholic Congress Report, pp. 85–90.

'Jesus the Messiah' in G.K.A. Bell and A. Deissmann (eds), *Mysterium Christi*, London, pp. 69–89.

Review of C.A. Anderson-Scott, *New Testament Ethics — An Introduction*; *The Call for Christian Unity: The Challenge of a World Situation* (a volume of essays contributed at the request of the Anglican Evangelical Group Movement); M. Pribilla, S.J., *Um Kirchliche Einheit — Stockholm, Lausanne, Rome*, *J.T.S.*, XXXI, pp. 411–5.

Review of J.H. Bernard, *A Critical and Exegetical Commentary on the Gospel according to St John*, *Theology*, XX, pp. 165–71.

1931

'The Incarnate Christ', *The Sign*, August.
The Riddle of the New Testament, with F.N. Davey, London.

1932

Review of R.B. Hoyle, *The Teaching of Karl Barth*, *J.T.S.*, XXXIII,
pp. 204–6.

1933

Translation of K. Barth, *The Epistle to the Romans*, Oxford.
'A Theological Lexicon to the New Testament', review article on G. Kittel
(ed.), *Theologisches Worterbuch zum Neuen Testament*, *Theology* XXVI,
pp. 82–7.

1936

'The Rediscovery of Abraham', review of Sir Leonard Woolley,
Abraham — Recent Discoveries and Hebrew Origins, *The London Mercury*,
April, pp. 636f.

1938

Cambridge Sermons, London, with introduction by C,H. Smyth.

1940

The Fourth Gospel, 2 vols, ed. F.N. Davey; 1-vol. edition, 1947.

1960

We are the Pharisees. . ., London. A collection of sermons, comprising two
courses: 'Contemporary Judaism' and 'Studying the Bible'.

1981

*Crucifixion-Resurrection: The Pattern of the Theology and Ethics of the New
Testament*, with F.N. Davey, and edited, with biographical introduction, by
G.S. Wakefield, London.

BIBLIOGRAPHY

Barbour, R.S., 'Biblical Classics X: Karl Barth The Epistle to the Romans', *Exp. T.*, XC, 1979, pp. 264–8.

Barmann, L.F., *Baron Friedrich von Hügel and the Modernist Crisis in England*, Cambridge, 1972.

Barr, J., *Explorations in Theology 7: The Scope and Authority of the Bible*, London, 1980.

——, *Fundamentalism*, London, 1977.

——, *The Semantics of Biblical Language*, Oxford, 1961.

Barrett, C.K., 'Albert Schweitzer and the New Testament', *Exp. T.*, LXXXVII, 1975, pp. 4–10.

——, *A Commentary on the Epistle to the Romans*, London, 1957.

——, *Essays on John*, London, 1982.

——, *The Gospel according to St. John*, 1st edn, London, 1955; 2nd edn, London, 1978.

——, *The Gospel of John and Judaism*, London, 1975.

——'The Prologue of St. John's Gospel' (Ethel M. Wood Lecture, 1970) in *New Testament Essays*, London, 1972, pp. 27–48.

——, *Jesus and the Gospel Tradition*, London, 1967.

Bell, G.K.A., and A. Deissmann (ed.), *Mysterium Christi*, London, 1930.

Bernard, J.H., *A Critical and Exegetical Commentary on the Gospel according to St. John*, 2 vols, Edinburgh, 1928.

Bezzant, J.S., review of *The Riddle of the New Testament*, *The Modern Churchman*, XXI, 1931–2, pp. 206–10.

Bowden, J., *Karl Barth*, London, 1971.

Brabazon, J., *Albert Schweitzer: A Comprehensive Biography*, London, 1971.

Bultmann, R., *The Gospel of John*, Eng. transl. Oxford, 1973.

——, *The History of the Synoptic Tradition*, Eng. transl. Oxford, 1963.

——, *Jesus Christ and Mythology*, New York, 1958.

——, *Jesus and the Word*, Eng. transl. London, 1934; references are to 1958 edn).

——, *Theology of the New Testament*, Eng. transl. London, vol. 1, 1952; vol. 2, 1955.

Burkitt, F.C., 'The Eschatological Idea in the Gospel', *Cambridge Biblical Essays*, Cambridge, 1909, pp. 193–213.

Bury, P., *The College of Corpus Christi and the Blessed Virgin Mary: A History from 1822-1952*, Cambridge, 1952.

Busch, E., *Karl Barth: His Life from Letters and Autobiographical Texts*, Eng. transl. London, 1976.

Carpenter, J., *Gore: A Study in Liberal Catholic Thought*, London, 1960.

Cave, S., review of K. Barth, *Romans*, *J.T.S.*, XXXIV, 1933, pp. 412–6.

Childs, B.S., *Biblical Theology in Crisis*, Philadelphia, 1970.

Cobham, J.O., 'E.C. Hoskyns: The Sunderland Curate', *C.Q.R.*, CLVIII, 1957, pp. 280–95.

—, 'Hoskyns, Sir Edwyn Clement', *D.N.B. 1931–40*, Oxford, 1949, pp. 448f.

—, 'Sir Edwyn Hoskyns on Justification by Faith: His course of sermons on "The XXXIX Articles": ', *C.Q.R.*, CLIX, 1958, pp. 325–40.

Cowling, M., *Religion and Public Doctrine in Modern England*, Cambridge, 1980.

Cranfield, C.E.B., *A Critical and Exegetical Commentary on the Epistle to the Romans*, 2 vols, Edinburgh, 1975.

Creed, J.M., review of *Cambridge Sermons, J.T.S.*, XL., 1939, pp. 209–11.

Dibelius, M., *From Tradition to Gospel*, Eng. transl. London, 1934.

Dillistone, F.W., *Charles Dodd: Interpreter of the New Testament*, London, 1977.

—, *Charles Raven: Naturalist, Historian, Theologian*, London, 1975.

Dodd, C.H., *Historical Tradition in the Fourth Gospel*, Cambridge, 1963.

—, *The Interpretation of the Fourth Gospel*, Cambridge, 1953.

—, Review of E.C. Hoskyns, *The Fourth Gospel, Theology*, XLI, 1940, pp. 305–10.

Downing, F.G., *The Church and Jesus: A Study in History, Philosophy and Theology*, S.B.T., 2nd series, 10, London, 1968.

Dunn, J.D.G., *Unity and Diversity in the New Testament*, London, 1977.

Ebeling, G., 'The Meaning of Biblical Theology', *J.T.S.*, new series, VI, 1955, pp. 210–25.

Ericksen, R., 'Theology in the Third Reich: The Case of Gerhard Kittel', *J.C.H.*, 12, 1977, pp. 595–622.

Evans, C.F., 'Christ at Prayer in St John's Gospel', *The Kingsman*, 12, 1969–70, pp. 9–20.

—, 'Crucifixion-Resurrection: Some Reflections on Sir Edwyn Hoskyns as Theologian', *Epworth Review*, 10, 1983, pp. 70–6 and 79–86.

—, 'The Eucharist and Symbolism in the New Testament', *Thinking about the Eucharist*, London, 1972, pp. 59–66.

—, *Explorations in Theology 2*, London, 1977.

—, 'The Faith of an Exegete', *Theology*, LXXVII, 1974, pp. 287–90.

—, 'I will go before you into Galilee', *J.T.S.*, new series, V, 1954, pp. 3–18.

—, *Resurrection and the New Testament*, S.B.T., 2nd series, 12, London, 1970.

—, Review of R. Bultmann, *The Gospel of John*, *S.J.T.*, 26, 1973, pp. 341–9.

Fenton, J.C., *The Gospel according to John*, Oxford, 1970.

Fuller, R.H., *The New Testament in Current Study*, London, 1963.

Gardner-Smith, P., 'The last fifty years of Cambridge Theology: An informal Retrospect', *Cambridge Review*, 9 Oct. 1954, pp. 23–6 and 43.

Gutteridge, R., 'German Protestantism and the Hitler Regime', *Theology*, XXVII, 1933, pp. 243–64.

—, *Open thy Mouth for the Dumb! The German Evangelical Church and the Jews, 1879–1950*, Oxford, 1976.

—, 'Sir Edwyn Hoskyns (1884–1937) — Wegbereiter, Bruckenbauer, Interpret', *Kerygma und Dogma*, 10, 1964, pp. 48–60.

Harnack, A., *What is Christianity?*, Eng. transl. London, 1904.

Herbert, G., *Fundamentalism and the Church of God*, London, 1957.

Hengel, M., *Between Jesus and Paul*, London, 1983.

——, *The Son of God*, London, 1976.

The Holy Bible: Its Authority and Message, part of the Report of the Lambeth Conference, London, 1958.

Hooker, M.D., 'Christology and Methodology', *N.T.S.*, 17, 1971, pp. 480–7.

——, 'In his own Image' in M.D. Hooker and C.J.A. Hickling (eds), *What about the New Testament? Essays in honour of Christopher Evans*, London, 1975, pp. 28–44.

——, 'On Using the Wrong Tool', *Theology*, LXXV, 1972, pp. 570–81.

——, *The Son of Man in Mark*, London, 1967.

Hopkins, G.G., 'Francis Noel Davey', *Theology*, LXXVI, 1973, pp. 225–7.

Howard, W.F., *The Fourth Gospel in Recent Criticism and Interpretation*, rev. edn by C.K. Barrett, London, 1955.

——, Review of E.C. Hoskyns, *The Fourth Gospel*, *J.T.S.*, XLII, 1941, pp. 75–81.

Howarth, T.E.B., *Cambridge between Two Wars*, London, 1978.

Hunter, A.M., *According to John*, London, 1968.

——, *Interpreting the New Testament, 1900–1950*, London, 1951.

Jasper, R.C.D., *George Bell, Bishop of Chichester*, Oxford, 1967.

Kasemann, E., *The Testament of Jesus*, Eng. transl. London, 1976.

Kemp, E.W., *The Life and Letters of Kenneth Escott Kirk, Bishop of Oxford 1937–1954*, London, 1959.

Kittel, G., 'Lexiographia Sacra', Theology Occasional Papers, London, 1938.

Knox, W.L., and A.R. Vidler, *The Development of Modern Catholicism*, London, 1933.

Kümmel, W.G., *The New Testament: The History of the Investigation of its Problems*, Eng. transl. London, 1973.

Lightfoot, R.H., *The Gospel Message of St Mark*, Oxford, 1950.

——, *History and Interpretation in the Gospels* (Bampton Lectures, 1934), London, 1935.

——, *Locality and Doctrine in the Gospels*, London, 1938.

——, *St John's Gospel: A Commentary*, Oxford, 1956.

Lindars, B., *The Gospel of John*, London, 1972.

Lloyd, R., *The Church of England, 1900–1965*, London, 1966.

Loisy, A.F., *The Gospel and the Church*, Eng. transl. London, 1908.

MacKinnon, D.M., 'Tillich, Frege, Kittel: Some Reflections on a Dark Theme'. *Explorations in Theology 5*, London, 1979, pp. 129–37.

——, 'Revised Reviews: XIII — Barth's Epistle to the Romans', *Theology*, LXV, 1962, pp. 3–7.

——, 'Oliver Chase Quick as a Theologian' (an unpublished tribute).

Marshall, I., *The Origins of New Testament Christology*, Illinois, 1976.

Morgan, R., *The Nature of New Testament Theology*, S.B.T., 2nd series, 25, London, 1975.

Morris, L., *The Gospel according to John*, London, 1971.

Moule, C.F.D., *The Birth of the New Testament*, London, 1962.

——, *New Testament Interpretation*, Cambridge, 1982.

——, *The Origins of Christology*,Cambridge, 1977.

——, *The Phenomenon of the New Testament*, S.B.T., 2nd series, 1, London, 1967.

——, 'Revised Reviews: IV — Sir Edwyn Hoskyns and Noel Davey: The Riddle of the New Testament', *Theology*, LXIV, 1961, pp. 144–6.

Mozley, J.K., *Some Tendencies in British Theology*, London, 1951.

Narborough, F.D.V., review of *The Riddle of the New Testament*, *C.Q.R.*, CXIV, 1932, pp. 304–8.

Neill, S., *The Interpretation of the New Testament 1861–1961*, Oxford, 1966.

Nineham, D.E., *Explorations in Theology 1*, London, 1977.

——, 'The Use of the Bible in Modern Theology', *B.J.R.L.*, LII, 1969–70, pp. 178–99.

Perrin, N., *The Kingdom of God in the Teaching of Jesus*, London, 1963.

Porter, J.R., 'The Case of Gerhard Kittel', *Theology*, L, 1947, pp. 401–6.

Quick, O.C., *The Gospel of Divine Action*, London, 1933.

Ramsey, A.M., 'The Apostolic Age and Our Own' and 'The Historical Jesus and the Christian Faith', *Canterbury Pilgrim*, London, 1974.

——, *God, Christ and the World: A Study in Contemporary Theology*, London, 1969.

——, *The Gospel and the Catholic Church*, London, 1936.

——, *From Gore to Temple*, London, 1960.

——, *Jesus and the Living Past*, Oxford, 1980.

——, *The Glory of God and the Transfiguration of Christ*, London, 1949.

——, *The Resurrection of Christ*, London, 1945.

Reardon, B.M.G., *From Coleridge to Gore*, London, 1971.

——, *Liberal Protestantism*, London, 1968.

——, *Liberalism and Tradition: Aspects of Catholic Thought in Nineteenth Century France*, Cambridge, 1975.

——, *Roman Catholic Modernism*, London, 1970.

Richardson, A., 'The Rise of Modern Biblical Scholarship' in S.L. Greenslade (ed.), *Cambridge History of the Bible*, vol. 3, Cambridge, 1963, pp. 294–338.

Robbins, K., 'Martin Niemoller: the German Church Struggle and English Opinion', *J.E.H.*, XXI, 1970, pp. 149–70.

Robinson, J.A.T., *Twelve New Testament Studies*, S.B.T., 1st series, 14, London, 1962.

Schweitzer, A., *The Quest of the Historical Jesus*, Eng. transl. London, 1908.

Seaver, G., *Albert Schweitzer: The Man and his Mind*, London, 1948.

Selwyn, E.G. (ed.), *Essays Catholic and Critical*, London, 1926.

——, review of *The Riddle of the New Testament*, *Theology*, XXIII, 1931, pp. 229–31.

Simon, U.E., *Sitting in Judgement: 1913–1963*, London, 1978.

Smalley, S.S., *John — Evangelist and Interpreter*, Exeter, 1978.

Smart, J.D., *The Interpretation of Scripture*, London, 1961.

—— (ed.), *Revolutionary Theology in the Making*, London, 1964.

Smyth, C.H., 'In Memoriam: Canon Sir Edwyn Hoskyns, 1884–1937', *Theology*, XXXV, 1937, pp. 135–41.

——, 'A Page from the Past', *Theology*, LXXVI, 1973, pp. 645–52.

——, 'Westcott, Hort and Hoskyns', *Cambridge Review*, 1 Feb. 1947.

Spens, W., *Belief and Practice*, London, 1915.

Stanton, G.N., 'Form Criticism Revisited' in M.D. Hooker and C.J.A. Hickling (eds), *What about the New Testament? Essays in honour of Christopher Evans*, London, 1975, pp. 13–27.

Stephenson, A.M.G., 'The Bible and Lambeth Conferences', *Theology*, LXXVIII, 1975, pp. 361–70.

Stuhlmacher, P., 'Adolf Schlatter's Interpretation of Scripture', *N.T.S.*, 24, 1978, pp. 433–46.

Tasker, R.V.G., review of E.C. Hoskyns, *The Fourth Gospel*, *C.Q.R.*, CXXX, 1940, pp. 318–20.

Torrance, T.F., *Karl Barth: An Introduction to his Early Theology, 1910–1931*, London, 1962.

Tyrrell, G., *Christianity at the Cross Roads*, London, 1909 (references are to the 1963 edn).

Vidler, A.R., *20th Century Defenders of the Faith*, London, 1965.

——, *Essays in Liberality*, London, 1957.

——, *The Modernist Movement in the Roman Church: Its Origins and Outcome*, Cambridge, 1934.

——, *A Variety of Catholic Modernists*, Cambridge, 1970.

Wakefield, G.S., 'Hoskyns and Raven: The Theological Issue', *Theology*, LXXVIII, 1975, pp. 568–76.

——, *Robert Newton Flew, 1886–1962*, London, 1971.

——, 'Sir Edwyn Hoskyns: Biblical Theologian' (unpublished paper).

Weiss, J., *Jesus' Proclamation of the Kingdom of God*, Eng. transl. London, 1971.

Wiles, M.F., *The Spiritual Gospel: The Interpretation of the Fourth Gospel in the Early Church*, Cambridge, 1960.

INDEX

Allen, W.C., 10
Anderson, R., 9
Anglo-Catholicism, 1, 2, 3 n.4, 5, 7–9, 18–9, 21, 24, 27, 109

Bacon, B.W., 47
Balmforth, H., 68, 75 n.114
Barnes, E.C., 21, 24, 25 n.16
Barr, J., 64–5, 94 n.49, 95 n.57
Barrett, C.K., 3 n.1, 36, 9 n.2, 106, 109, 111, 125, 127, 129–32
Barth, K., 1, 13, 15 n.2, 98–101, 106–9, 111, 138–9
Bauer, W., 102, 115
Beginnings of Christianity, The, 12, 65
Bell, G.K.A., 55, 71 n.41, 141
Benoit, P., 124
Bernard, J., 102
Bethune-Baker, J.F., 9, 12–4, 71 n.49
Biblical theology 2, 13–14, 45, 87–9
Bicknell, E.G., 8, 19
Brown, R.E., 125
Bultmann, R., 36–7, 40 n.74, 43 n.104, 48, 66–7, 75 n.111, 86, 93 n.43, 115–16, 126–7, 130–1
Burkitt, F.C., 10, 14, 17 n.47, 43 nn.98 and 104, 66, 72 n.56, 91 n.13

Caldwell, R.T., 19
Calvin, J., 109
Cambridge University, 4, 13, 27, 62, 141
Carpenter, J.E., 47
Catholicism, 24, 29, 30, 33, 35, 48, 50, 60, 106
Catholic Modernism, 1, 6, 10, 15 n.13, 32–4, 44, 46–7, 60, 97
Charles, R.H., 9
Church of England, 4, 6, 10
Cobham, J.O., 3 n.1, 18, 44, 45, 69 nn.2 and 4
Cranfield, C.E.B., 76
Creed, J.M., 9, 16 n.32, 68, 74 nn.114 and 115
Cremer, H., 62, 74 n.80

Corpus Christi College, 1, 18, 25 nn.3 and 5, 65, 141

Davey, F.N., 1, 76, 90 n.1, 91 n.2, 98, 119
Dibelius, M., 48
Dodd, C.H., 57, 71 n.38, 72 n.56, 116–17, 122–3, 128, 130–2
Downing, F.G., 118
Dunn, J.D.G., 89, 94 n.59

Elliott-Binns, L.E., 9, 16 n.21
Evans, C.F., 15 n.1, 41 n.74, 71 n.40, 76, 91 n.1, 92 n.30

Fuller, R.H., 3 n.9, 106, 138

Gardner, P., 9, 10, 16 n.25
Gardner-Smith, P., 14, 17 n.46, 128
German theology, 2, 17, 44, 140
Girton Conference, 12, 17 n.39
Glover, T.R., 47
Gore, C., 5–6, 8, 10, 15 n.8, 52
Green, V.H.H., 13, 17 n.43
Guy, D.S., 65

Haitjema, T.L., 100
Harnack, A. von, 1, 16 n.20, 27–32, 34–5, 38 n.33, 47–8, 53, 60, 78, 80, 143
Harris, R., 9
Headlam, A.C., 10
Hermetic literature, 116–17
Holtzmann, H., 103
Hort, F.J.A., 14
Hoskyns, E.C.:
   His writings: *Christ and Catholicism* 3 n.4, 19, 21, 25 n.8, 46, 57, 92 n.33, 93 n.44; *Essays Catholic and Critical* 1, 6, 7, 8, 32, 33, 36, 46, 51, 69 n.5, 92 nn.33 and 35, 140; *Mysterium Christi* 1, 57, 70 n.38, 71 n.42, 72 n.55, 72 n.57, 72 n.66, 92 nn.15, 34 and 36, 93 n.44, 140; *The Riddle of the New Testament* 1, 44,

150

DATE DUE

OCT 17 2004			

HIGHSMITH #45230

Printed
in USA